Visual Perceptual Skill Building

written by
Raya Burstein

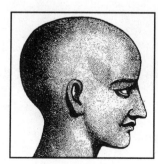

© 1998
CRITICAL THINKING BOOKS & SOFTWARE
www.criticalthinking.com
P.O. Box 448 • Pacific Grove • CA 93950-0448
Phone 800-458-4849 • FAX 831-393-3277
ISBN 0-89455-700-9
Printed in the United States of America

To my family,
who gave me support
and guidance
throughout the writing
of this book.

TABLE OF CONTENTS

INTRODUCTION

TO THE TEACHER OR THERAPIST

This is a visual perceptual workbook that includes exercises of the following types:
• Mazes
• Visual Discrimination
• Visual Closure
• Visual Figure Ground
• Visual Form Constancy
• Visual Memory
• Visual Sequential Memory
• Visual Spatial Relationship

Visual motor skills begin with the baby's learning to track objects. Once this essential function is mastered, the baby incorporates visual memory when he or she remembers the sight of the mother. More advanced skills such as the ones in this book are developed gradually, with a special emphasis on pre-reading and pre-writing development in K–2.

By the end of second grade, most students have mastered simple mazes and puzzles, write independently, and begin to enjoy reading for pleasure.

This book is intended for children in grades K–2 whose visual perceptual skills are developing. However, this book is also very useful in the rehabilitation of children and adults who are disabled with cerebral palsy or traumatic brain injury, are mentally or physically challenged or learning disabled, and anyone else who needs help in developing these skills.

Items 1–7 of each set are Easy; items 8–15 are Intermediate; and items 15–20 are Difficult. Each chapter has three pretest and three posttest items.

The exercises can be used as a follow-up activity for clients of all ages who have deficits in one or more areas as identified by the Motor Free Visual Perceptual Test (Colarusso and Hammill, 1972) or the Test of Visual Perceptual Skills (Gardner, 1982). These worksheets have been designed and used for remedial training for clients with cerebrovascular accidents, traumatic brain injury, cerebral palsy, mild mental retardation, and other conditions that affect the central nervous system and visual processing skills. Many clients with motoric dysfunction have delayed visual perceptual skills. During the course of normal development, the non-physically challenged child will incorporate visual and other sensory information through interaction and experience with the environment. Often, visual-perceptual problems of children and adults are recognized but not fully addressed in therapy, since the therapist focuses on motor problems, which are more obvious. Since people with disabilities may have difficulty in interacting with the environment successfully, they may have decreased opportunities for incorporating visual perceptual skills.

The following literature review focuses on visual perceptual skills as they develop in the child, but this developmental sequence can be applied to adults lacking such skills.

SENSORY INTEGRATION

It is important to show how different types of sensory information are integrated to form the appropriate functions a child needs (Ayres, 1979). Sensory integration is concerned with how sensation is perceived and organized and, ultimately, with how the adaptive response is brought about (Ayres, [1979], as cited in Moore, 1994). The essentials that a person needs in order to do academic work, work at a job, and be able to relate to family and friends are developed. The capacity for learning is a culmination of many years of development and integration in the brain. What does a child need to successfully get to that stage? What has hindered children who couldn't get there? The first requirement is appropriate stimulation of the senses and a continuous flow of impulses from receptors to the brain. The child with sensory integrative dysfunction generally meets this requirement. The failure is in sensory registration.

The sensory integrative process in life is fluid. The following senses—vestibular, proprioceptive and tactile—are then integrated to facilitate coordination of both sides of the body, body precept, attention span, motor planning, emotional stability, and activity level.

Touch sensations from every bit of skin come together for several types of use, including assisting the child in sucking and eating and helping form a mother-infant bond. Vestibular and proprioceptive senses contribute to well-organized eye movements, muscle tone, physical balance, posture, and gravitational security.

Visual perception is among the last skills a child develops. Eye-hand coordination is a prerequisite. Visual tracking in vertical, horizontal, diagonal, and circular planes is an essential precursor to visual perception. Visual perception consists of visual discrimination, visual figure ground, visual spatial relationships, visual form constancy, visual memory, and visual closure.

VISUAL PERCEPTION AND ACTIVITIES OF DAILY LIVING

Visual discrimination skills enhance a person's ability to perform his or her daily activities. For example, during dressing, a person uses figure-ground skills to select a garment from its background. Visual memory skills are needed when using a computer or augmentative communication device on the scanning mode to remember the location of the desired selection.

Visual tracking is used during feeding, dressing, and homemaking. The ability to complete a simple maze can make these tasks easier. Visual tracking is also essential in learning to read across a line and across a page.

Visual discrimination or matching skills are often used in sorting tasks for prevocational learning and letter discrimination in reading and spelling.

Visual sequential memory is used in higher level reading and numerical calculations and also for remembering phone numbers and addresses.

Visual closure is used when incomplete cues in the environment make visual completion of a form necessary, as in puzzles and games.

Visual form constancy is a skill needed for recognition of forms when they are smaller, bigger, or turned upside down. This is used during dressing, feeding, and hygiene tasks and also in letter and number recognition in reading and math.

Visual spatial relationships involve the orientation of objects in space and are used in activities of daily living such as dressing, feeding, communication, and homemaking. Academically, they affect visual organization on paper and following directions.

It is clear that using all of these skills to accomplish everyday tasks is essential to the well-being of the person. On the other hand, an individual who has difficulty in one or more areas of visual perception may experience interference with the performance of daily activities.

AUTHORS MENTIONED IN THE LITERATURE REVIEW

Colarusso, R.P. and Hammill, D. (1972) Motor Free Visual Perception Test. Academic Therapy, Novato.

Gardner, M.F. (1982). Test of Visual-Perceptual Skills (Non-Motor). Seattle: Washington Special Child Publications.

Ayres, A.J. (1979) Sensory Integration and the Child. 59-61. Los Angeles: Western Psychological Services

Moore, J. (1994) What Is Sensory Integration? Sensory Integration Special Interest Section Newsletter. Rockville: American Occupational Therapy Association, Vol. 17, #2

SOME DEFINITIONS

Visual spatial relationships—the ability to determine, from among four forms of identical configuration, the one single form or part of a single form that is going in a different direction from the other forms or from parts of forms

Visual sequential memory—the ability to remember for immediate recall (after a few seconds of exposure) a series of various forms from among four separate series of forms

Visual discrimination—the ability to match or determine exact characteristics

Visual memory—the ability to remember for immediate recall characteristics of a form

Visual form constancy—the ability to see a form and find that same form even though the form may be smaller or larger and, whatever the size, whether rotated, reversed and/or hidden among other forms

Visual figure ground—the ability to perceive a form visually; to find this form with other forms hidden in a conglomerated ground of matter

Visual motor skills—the ability to coordinate eye and hand movements to draw geometric shapes, letters, and numbers or to complete a maze

Visual perception—the ability to incorporate and process visual information; to perceive stimuli in forms that are recognized by the brain

Visual closure—the ability to recognize incomplete forms and "fill in" the lines mentally to match a completed form

USING THE PRETEST AND POSTTEST

Administer the three-example Pretest for each chapter before starting the program. Score a 1 for each example correctly answered. Score a 0 for each example with an incorrect answer. The Mazes should be scored as follows: 1 point for each example where the path drawn by the student is completely within the lines. Score 0 if the student's path is outside of the lines or if the student does not successfully complete the maze by going to the house. For example, score 0 if the student gets stuck at a roadblock. Score the subtests by adding up scores of 1, 2, and 3 for a possible total of 3 for each subtest. Total possible is 24.

To get an average score, divide the sum of subtest scores by 8. Review the results. If the student scores 3 on all items, no remedial training is indicated.

A score of 2, 1, or 0 on a subtest indicates remedial programming should be introduced for that chapter.

Sum of subtest score interpretation

24	—	No remedial program needed
19–24	—	Remedial program indicated in areas in which score is 2, 1, or 0. Start with some of the more challenging items from each chapter (items 15–20).
12–18	—	Remedial program indicated in areas in which score is 2, 1, or 0. Start with intermediate items from each chapter (items 8–14).
below 12	—	Remedial program indicated in areas in which score is 2, 1, or 0. Start with easy items for each chapter indicated (items 1–7).

Test Scores

Name _____

Test	Pretest Date	Posttest Date
Mazes		
Visual Discrimination		
Visual Closure		
Visual Figure Ground		
Visual Form Constancy		
Visual Memory		
Visual Sequential Memory		
Visual Spatial Relationships		
Sum of Subtests (Raw Score)		
Average Score (divide by 8)		

MAZES PRETEST

DIRECTIONS: Draw a line from the person to the house. Remember not to cross any lines.

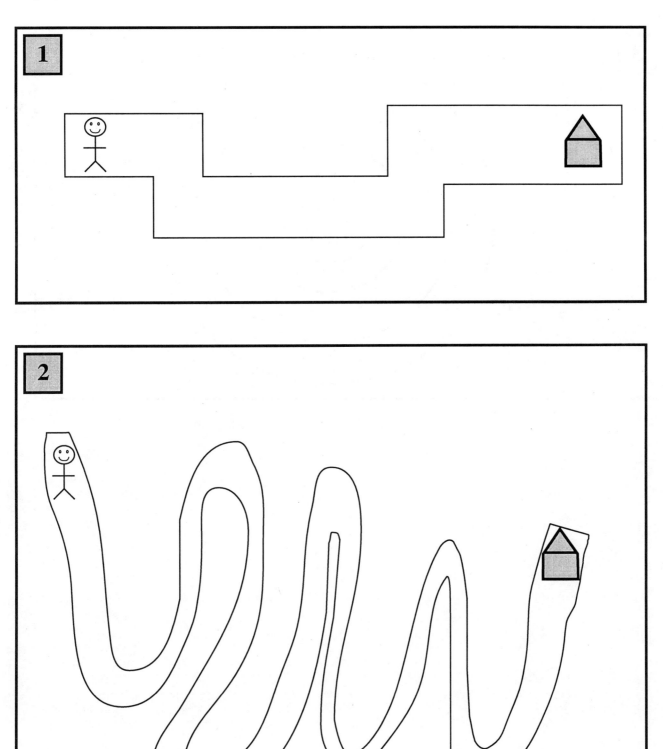

MAZES PRETEST

DIRECTIONS: Draw a line from the person to the house. Remember not to cross any lines.

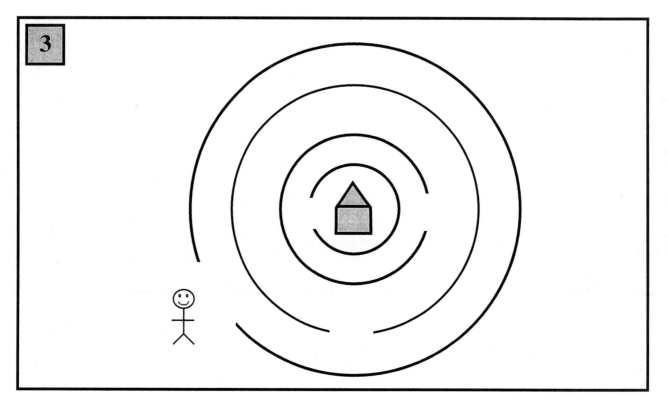

MAZES POSTTEST

DIRECTIONS: Draw a line from the person to the house. Remember not to cross any lines.

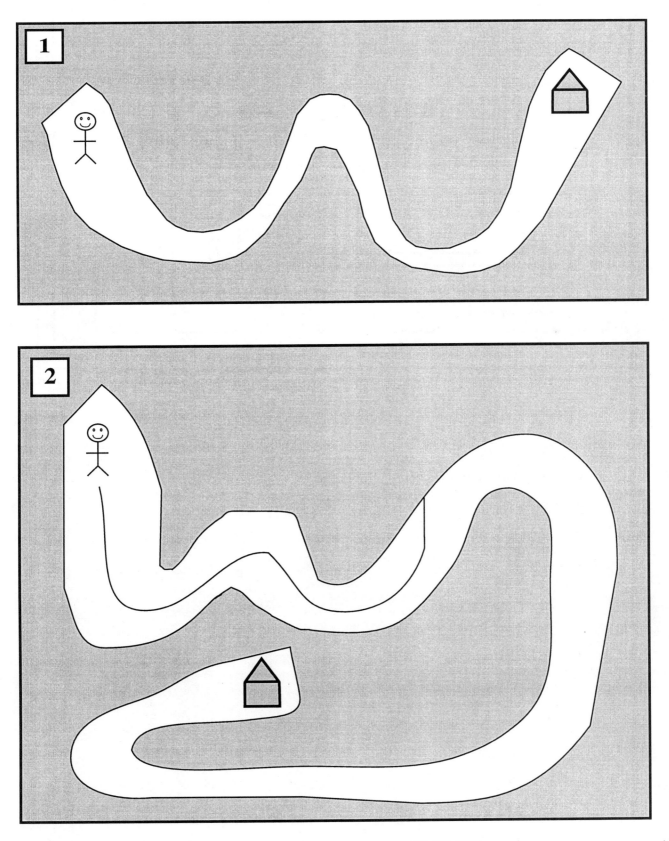

MAZES POSTTEST

DIRECTIONS: Draw a line from the person to the house. Remember not to cross any lines.

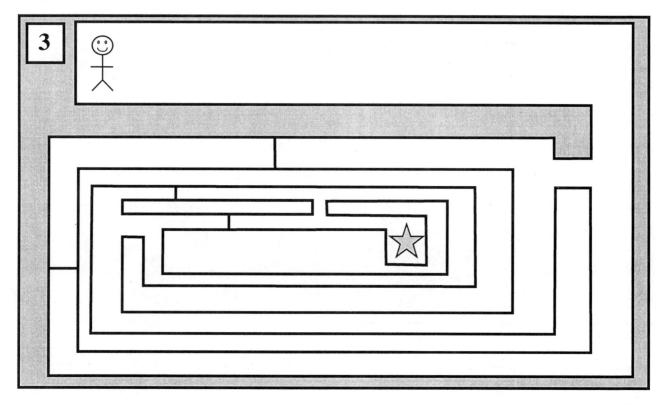

WORKING THROUGH A MAZE

DIRECTIONS: Draw a line from the person to the house or to the star. Remember not to cross any lines.

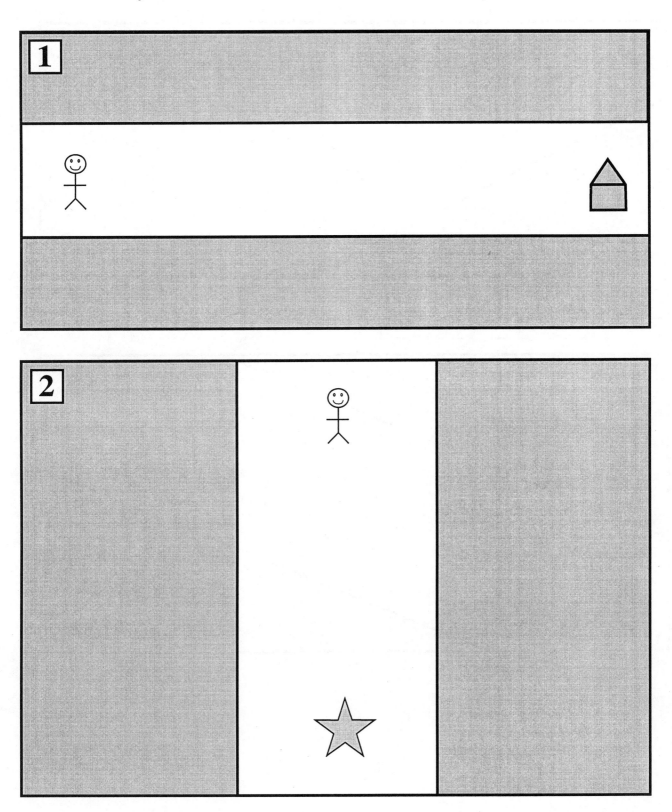

WORKING THROUGH A MAZE

DIRECTIONS: Draw a line from the person to the house. Remember not to cross any lines.

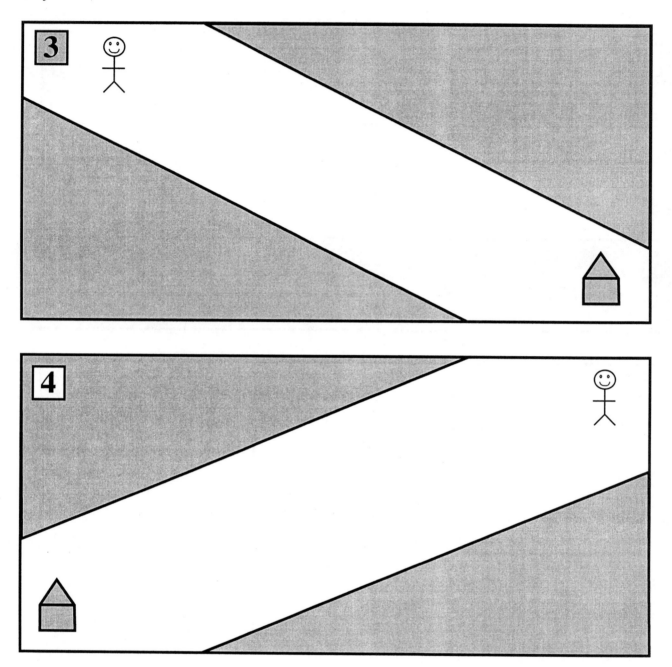

WORKING THROUGH A MAZE

DIRECTIONS: Draw a line from the person to the house or from the person to the star. Remember not to cross any lines.

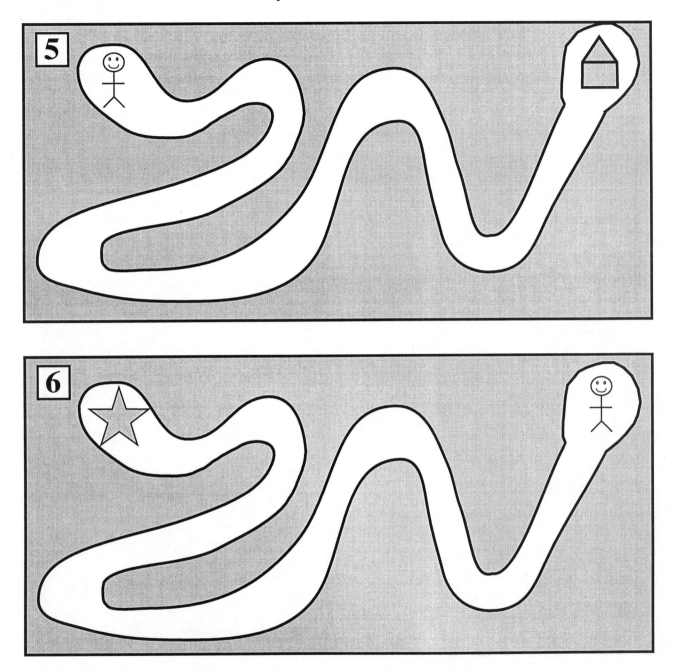

WORKING THROUGH A MAZE

DIRECTIONS: Draw a line from the person to the star. Remember not to cross any lines.

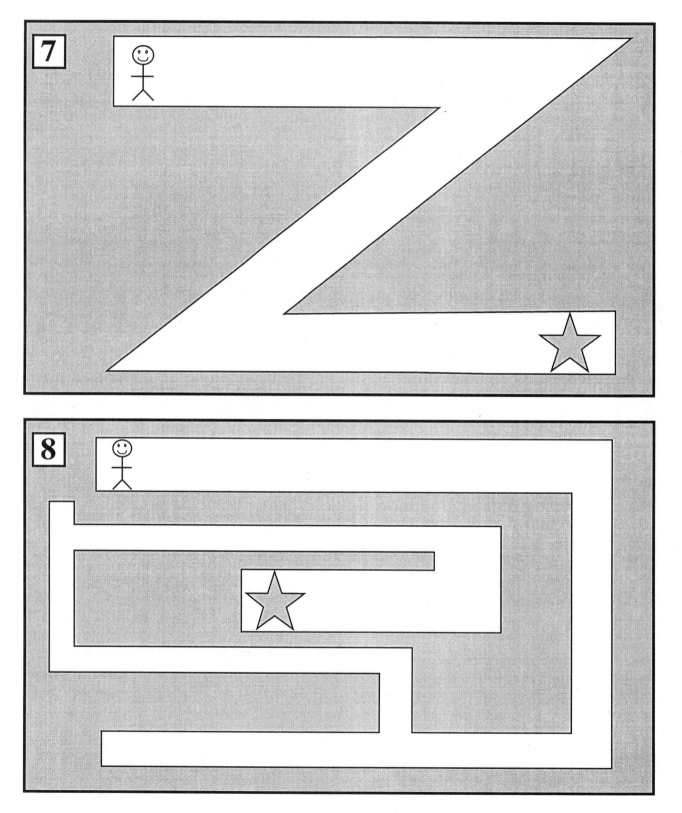

WORKING THROUGH A MAZE

DIRECTIONS: Draw a line from the person to the house. Remember not to cross any lines.

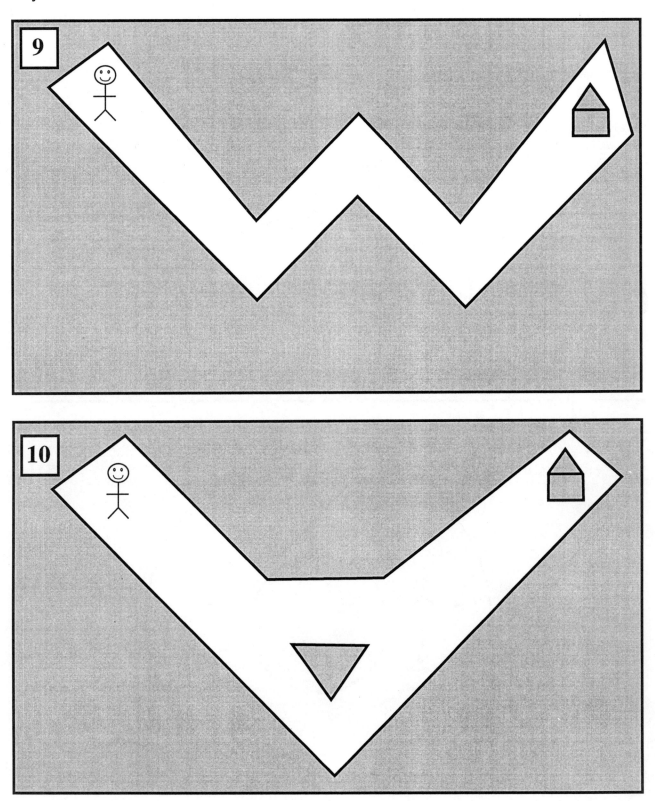

WORKING THROUGH A MAZE

DIRECTIONS: Draw a line from the person to the house or from the person to the star. Remember not to cross any lines.

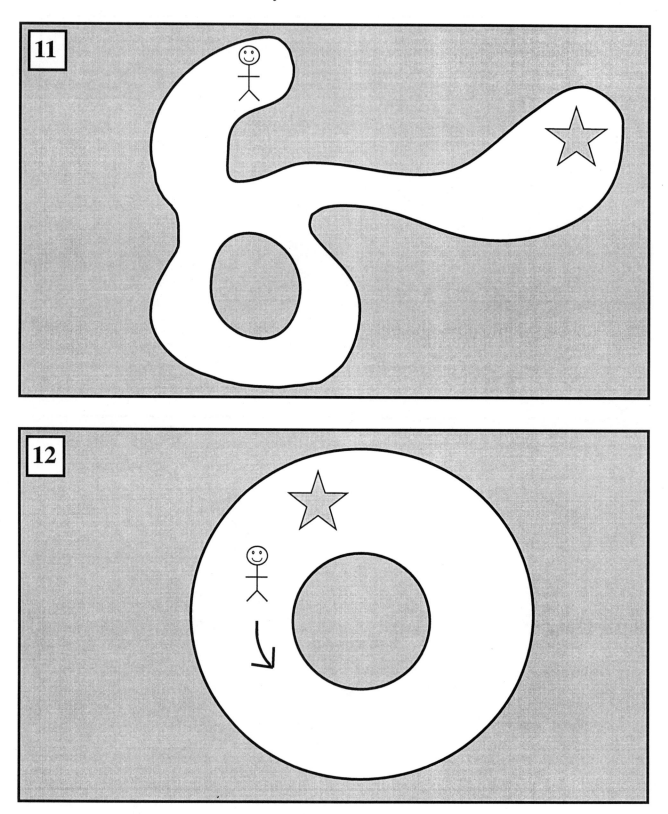

WORKING THROUGH A MAZE

DIRECTIONS: Draw a line from the person to the house or from the person to the star. Remember not to cross any lines.

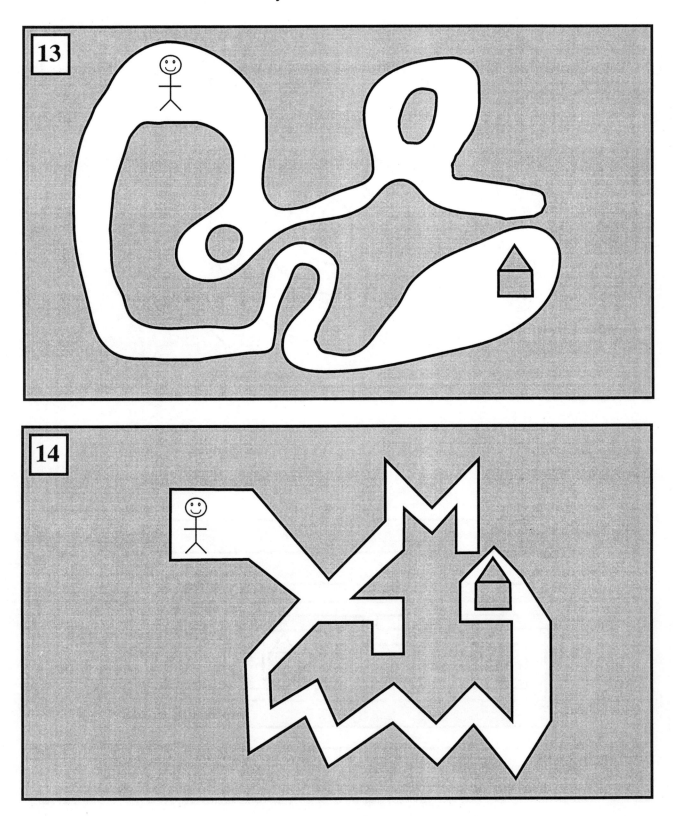

WORKING THROUGH A MAZE

DIRECTIONS: Draw a line from the person to the house. Remember not to cross any lines.

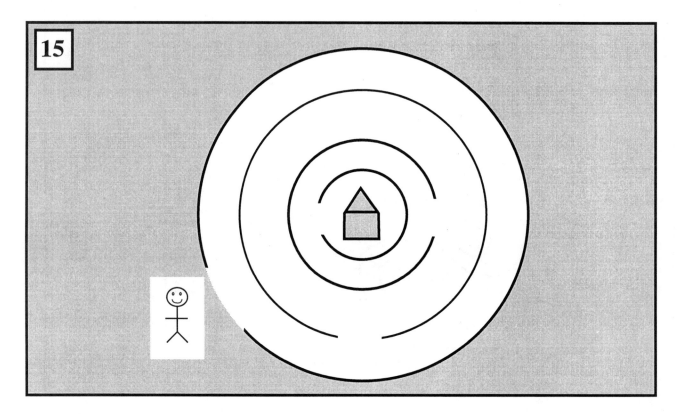

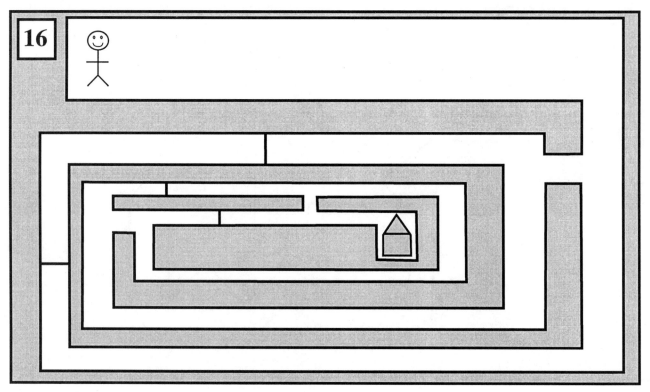

© 1998 CRITICAL THINKING BOOKS & SOFTWARE • WWW.CRITICALTHINKING.COM • 800-458-4849

WORKING THROUGH A MAZE

DIRECTIONS: Draw a line from the person to the house. Remember not to cross any lines.

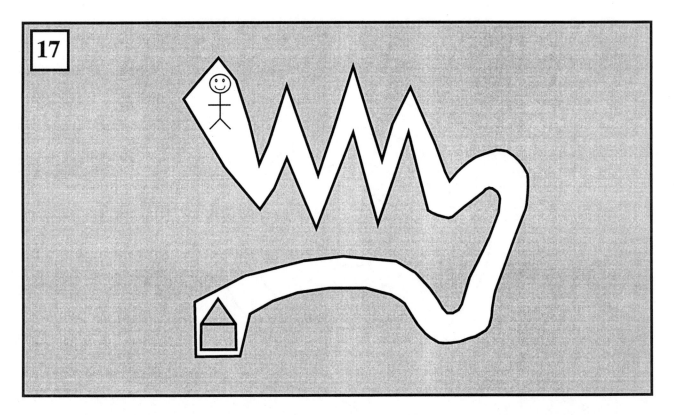

WORKING THROUGH A MAZE

DIRECTIONS: Draw a line from the person to the house. Remember not to cross any lines.

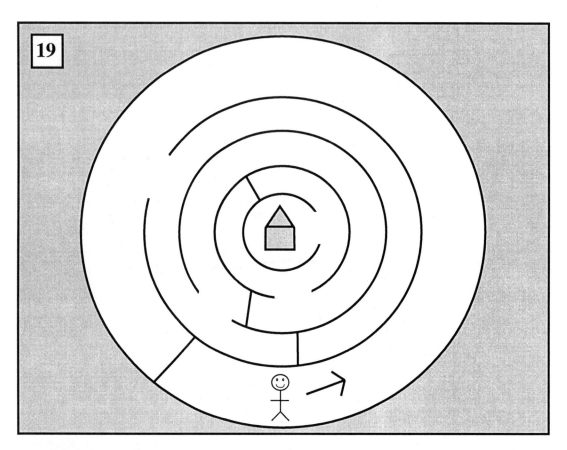

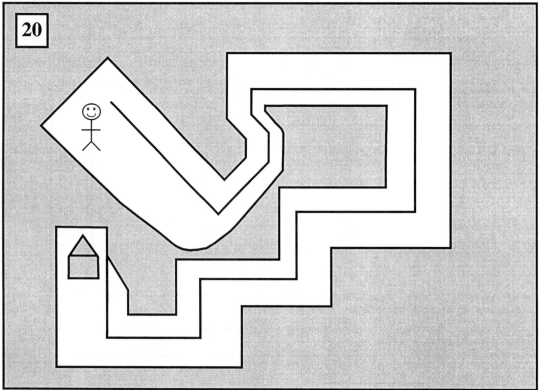

VISUAL DISCRIMINATION PRETEST

DIRECTIONS: Match the form on the top row to a form on the bottom row.

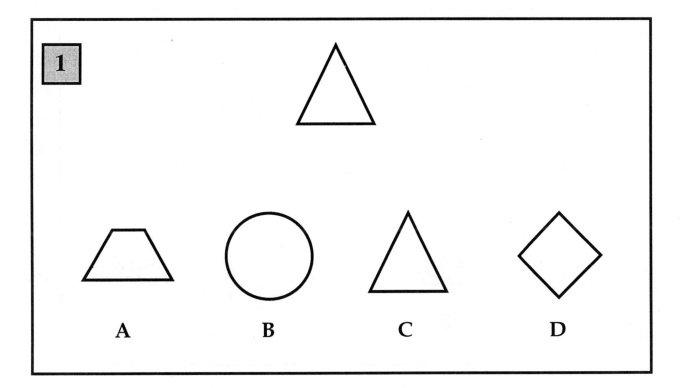

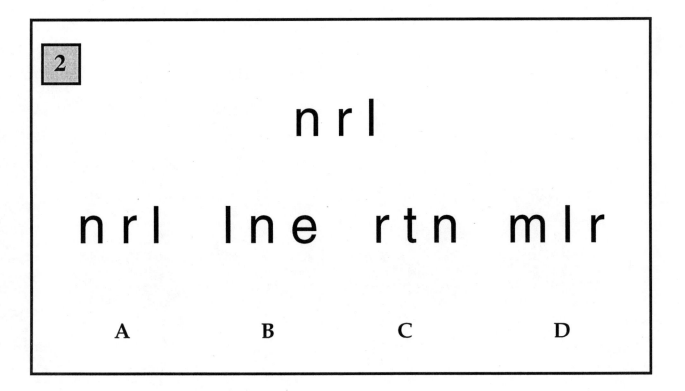

VISUAL DISCRIMINATION PRETEST

DIRECTIONS: Match the form on the top row to a form on the bottom row.

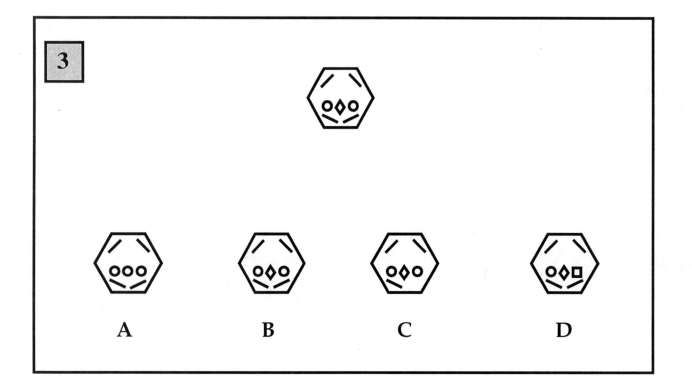

VISUAL DISCRIMINATION POSTTEST

DIRECTIONS: Match the form on the top row to a form on the bottom row.

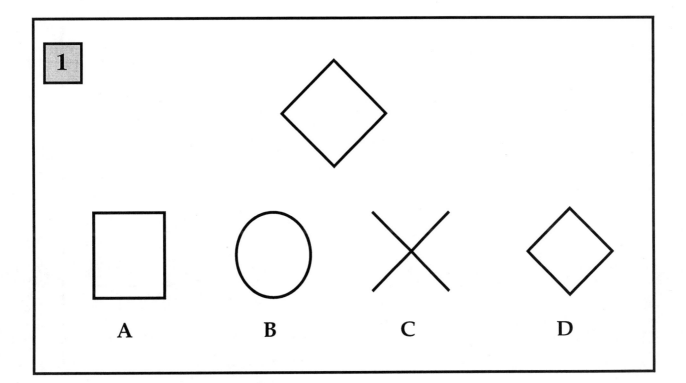

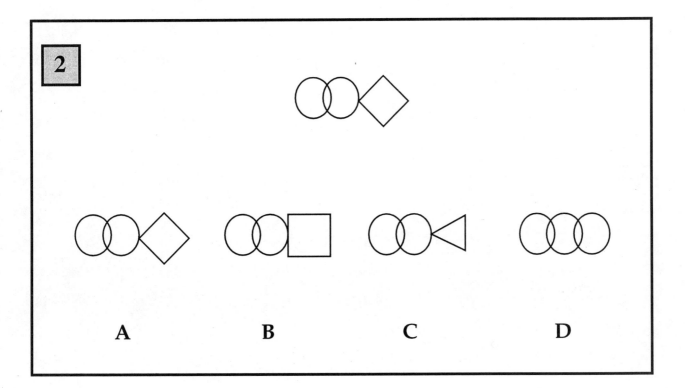

VISUAL DISCRIMINATION POSTTEST

DIRECTIONS: Match the form on the top row to a form on the bottom row.

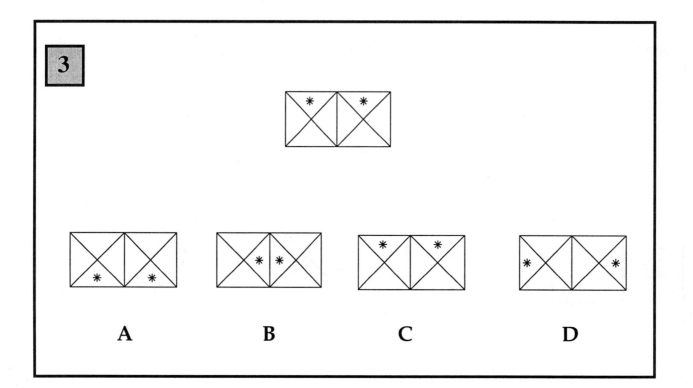

FINDING THE MATCHING SHAPE

DIRECTIONS: Match the form on the top row to a form on the bottom row.

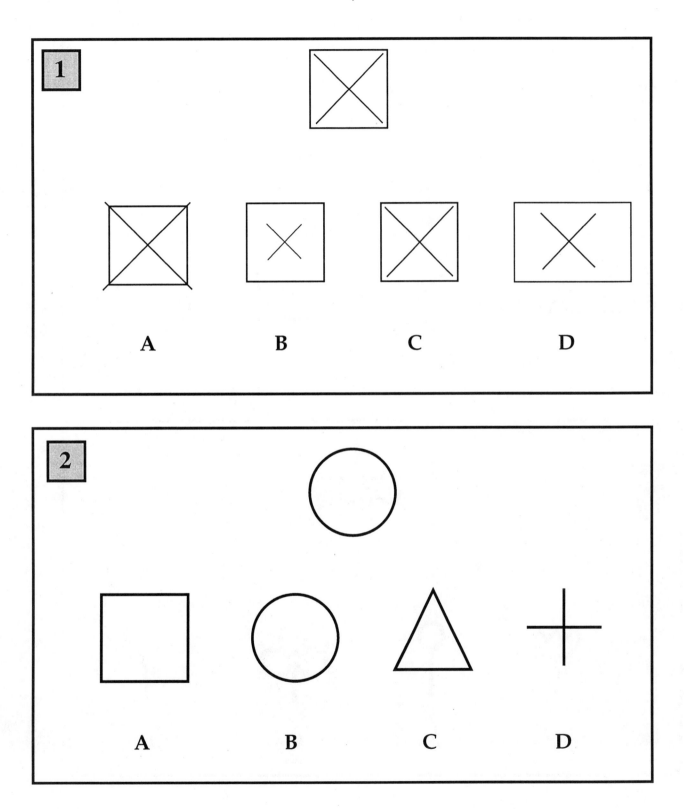

FINDING THE MATCHING SHAPE

DIRECTIONS: Match the form on the top row to a form on the bottom row.

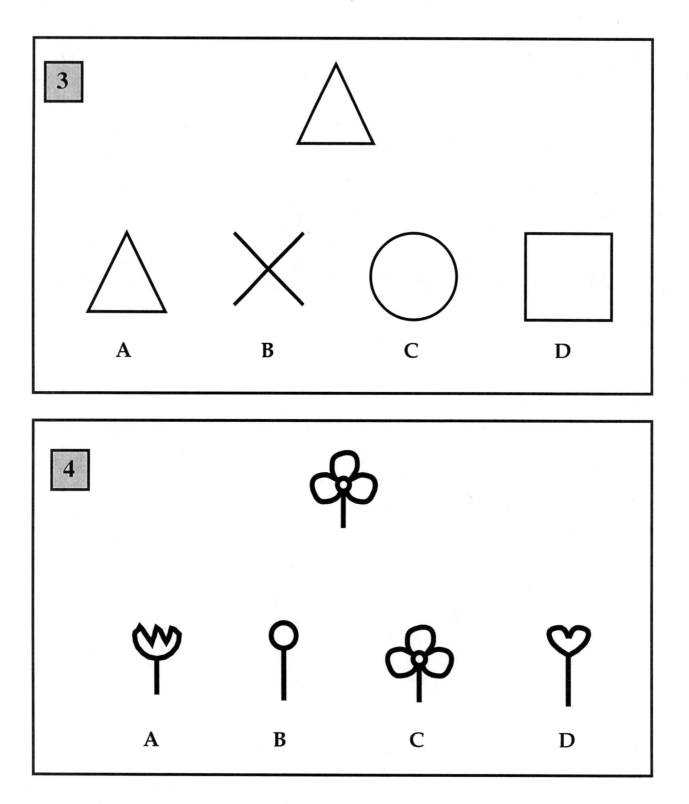

FINDING THE MATCHING SHAPE

DIRECTIONS: Match the form on the top row to a form on the bottom row.

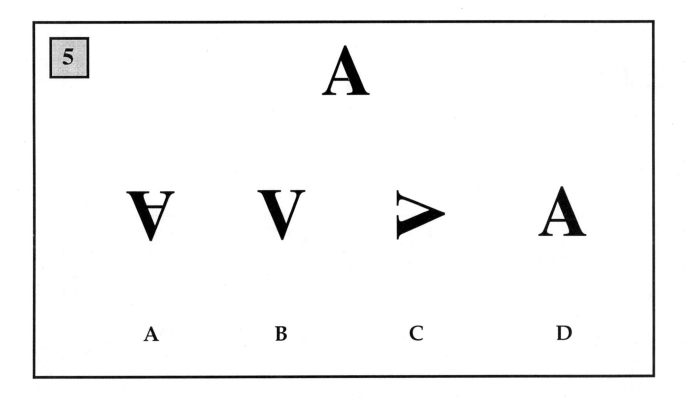

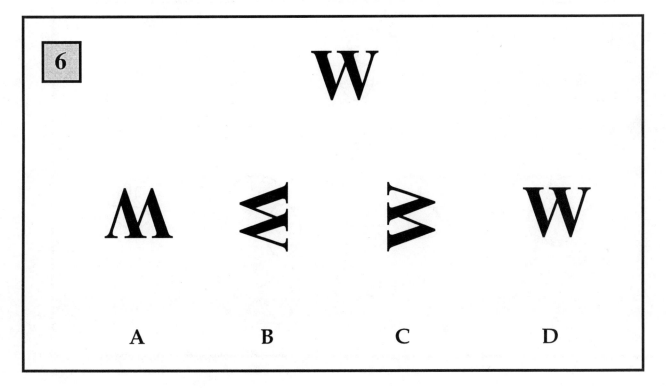

FINDING THE MATCHING SHAPE

DIRECTIONS: Match the form on the top row to a form on the bottom row.

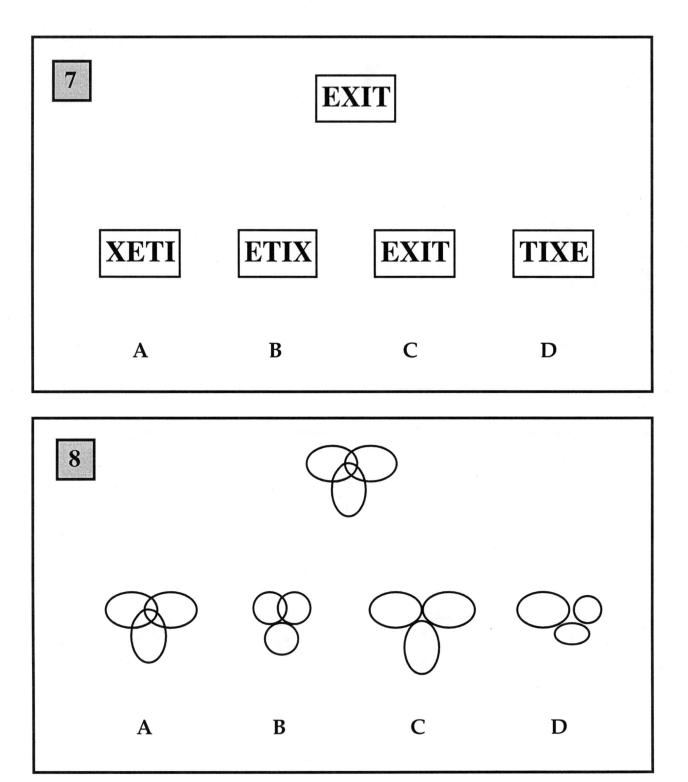

FINDING THE MATCHING SHAPE

DIRECTIONS: Match the form on the top row to a form on the bottom row.

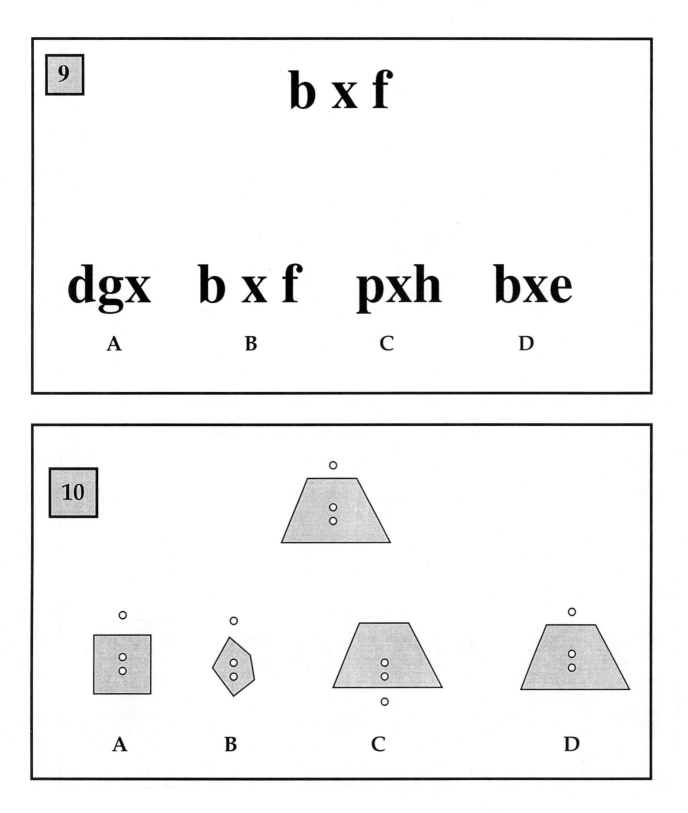

FINDING THE MATCHING SHAPE

DIRECTIONS: Match the form on the top row to a form on the bottom row.

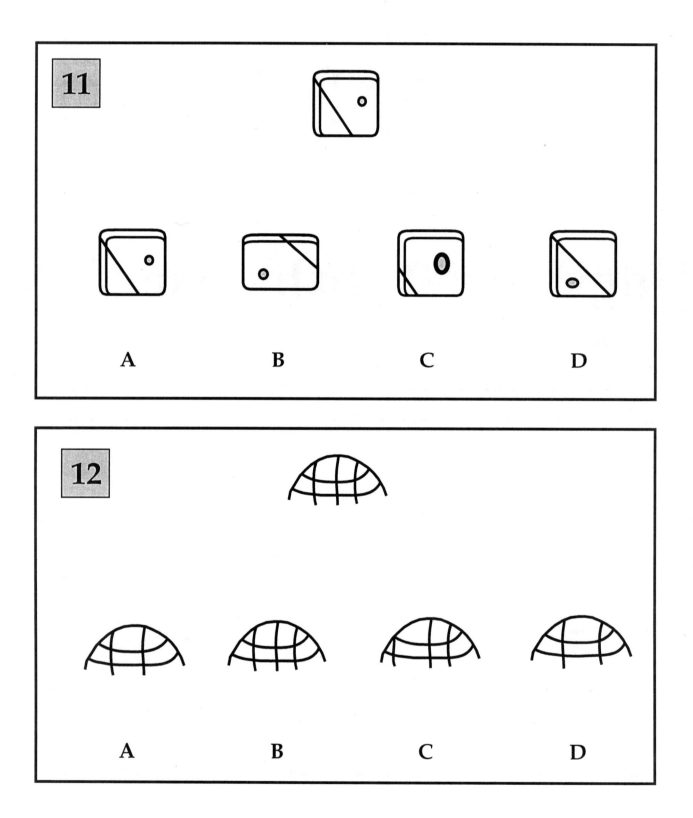

FINDING THE MATCHING SHAPE

DIRECTIONS: Match the form on the top row to a form on the bottom row.

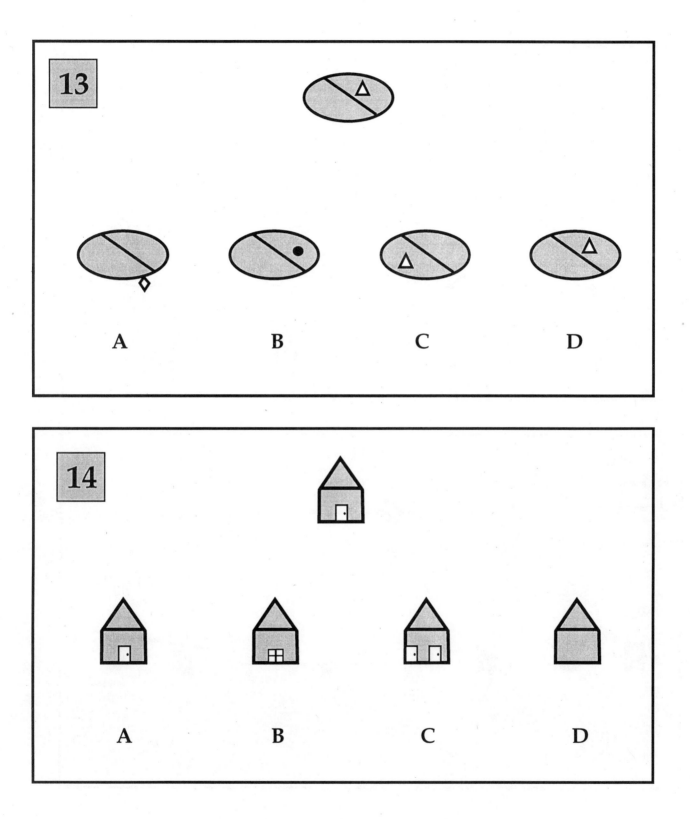

FINDING THE MATCHING SHAPE

DIRECTIONS: Match the form on the top row to a form on the bottom row.

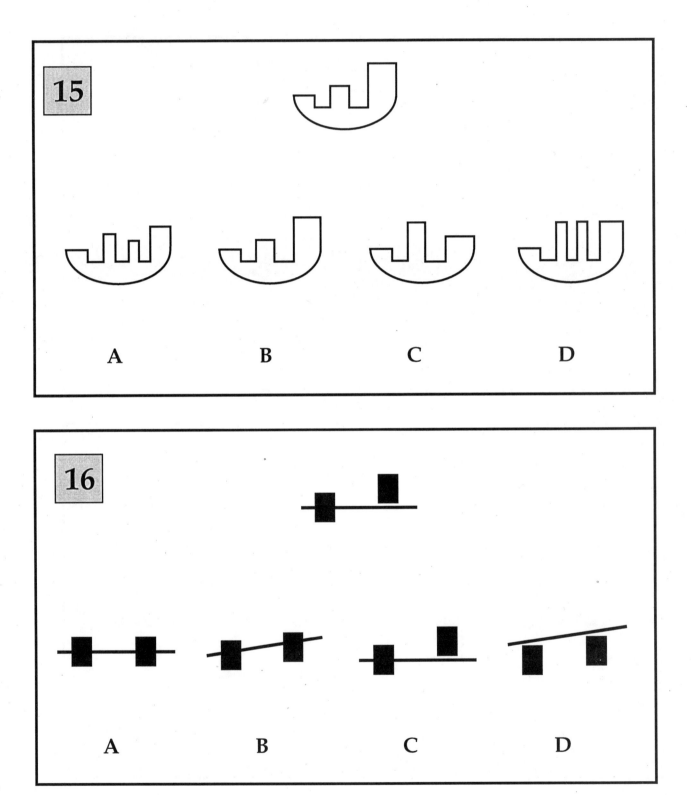

FINDING THE MATCHING SHAPE

DIRECTIONS: Match the form on the top row to a form on the bottom row.

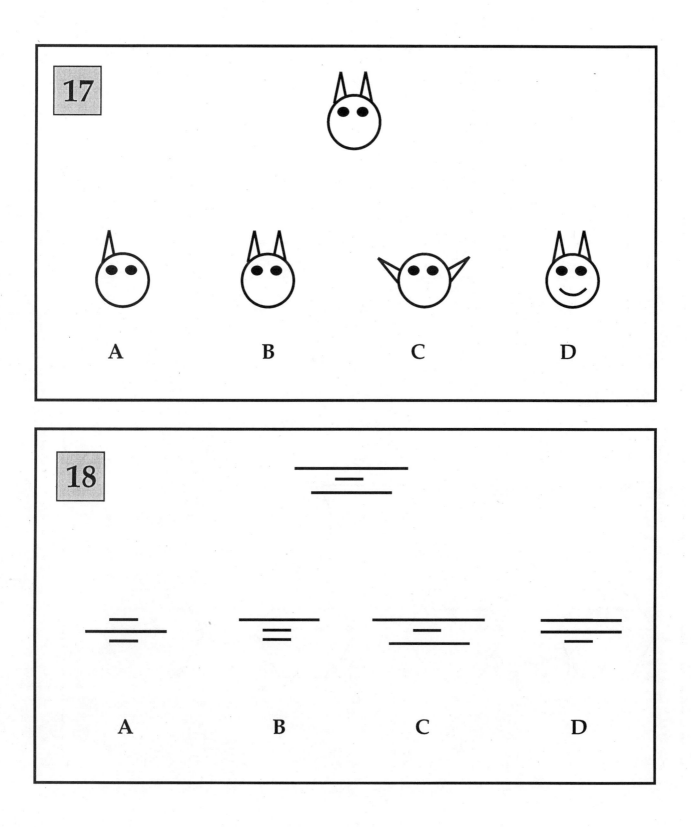

FINDING THE MATCHING SHAPE

DIRECTIONS: Match the form on the top row to a form on the bottom row.

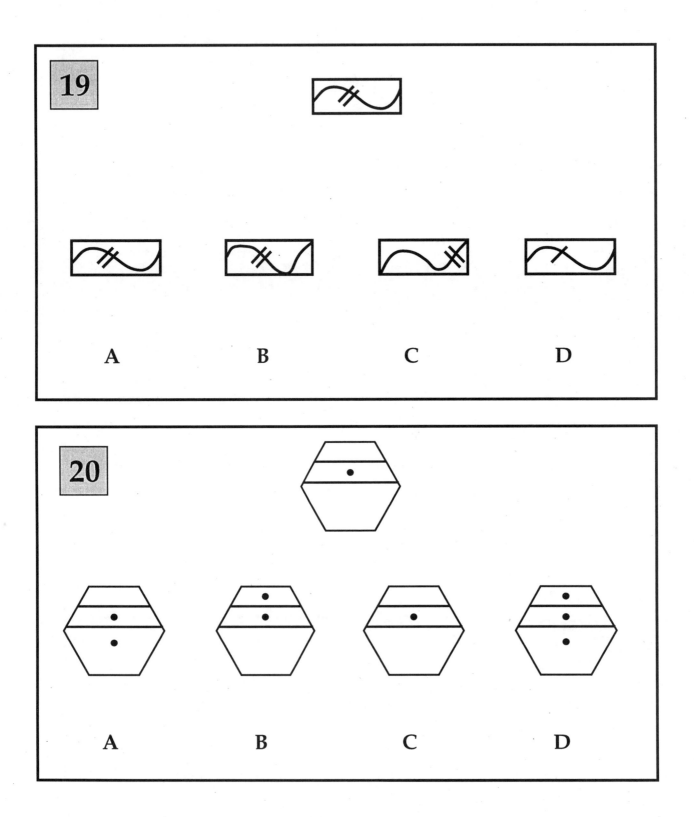

VISUAL CLOSURE PRETEST

DIRECTIONS: Match the incomplete form in the bottom row to its completed form in the top row.

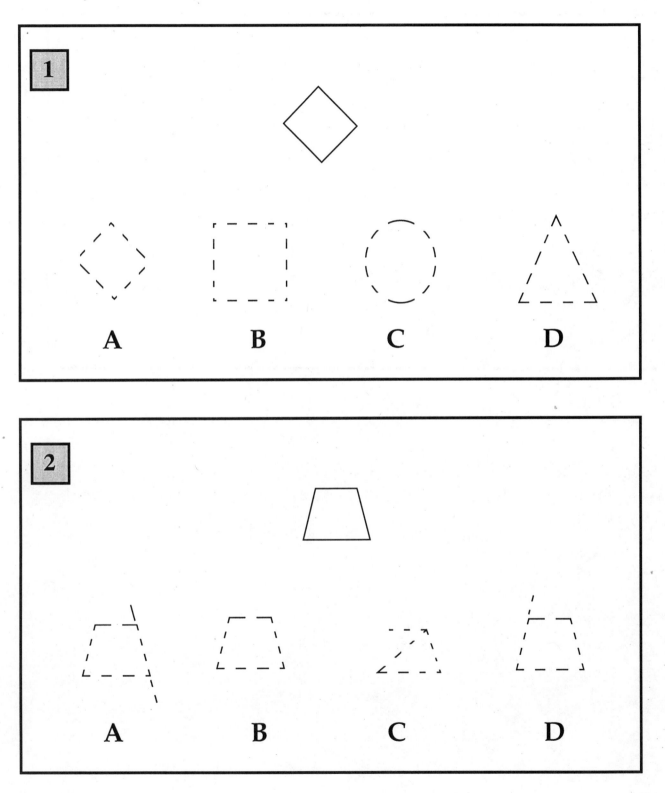

VISUAL CLOSURE PRETEST

DIRECTIONS: Match the incomplete form in the bottom row to its completed form in the top row.

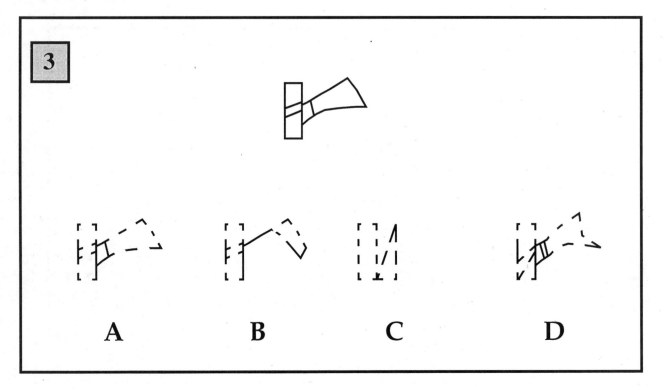

VISUAL CLOSURE POSTTEST

DIRECTIONS: Match the incomplete form in the bottom row to its completed form in the top row.

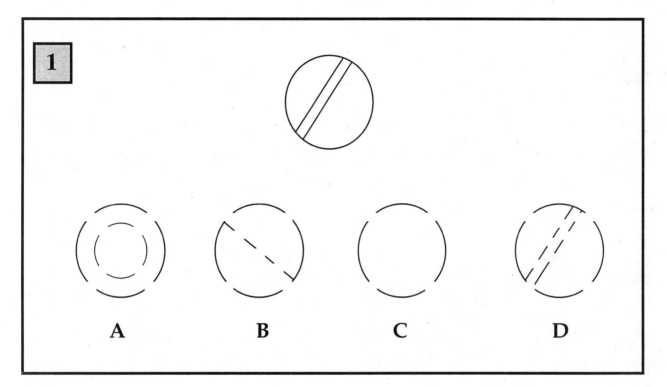

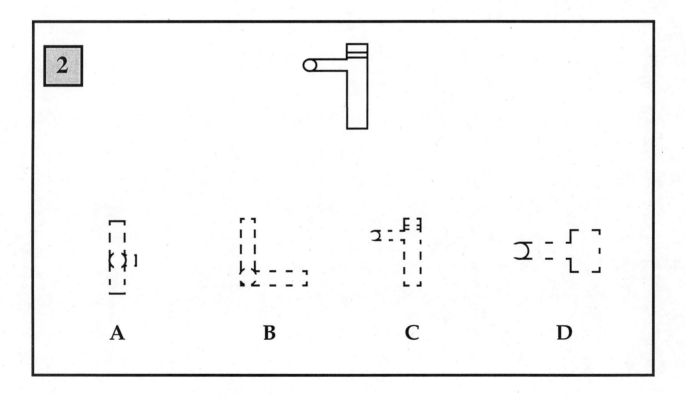

VISUAL CLOSURE POSTTEST

DIRECTIONS: Match the incomplete form in the bottom row to its completed form in the top row.

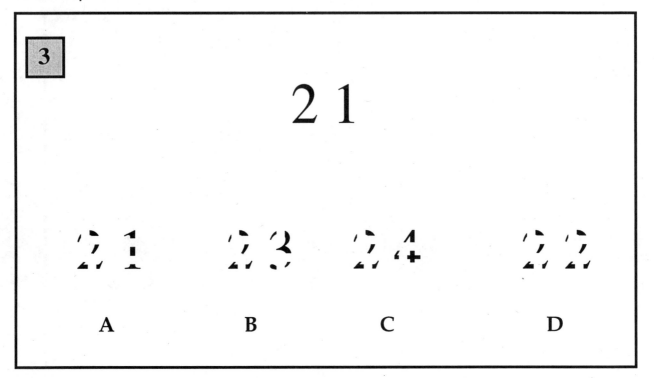

FINDING THE MATCHING SHAPE

DIRECTIONS: Match the incomplete form in the bottom row to its completed form in the top row.

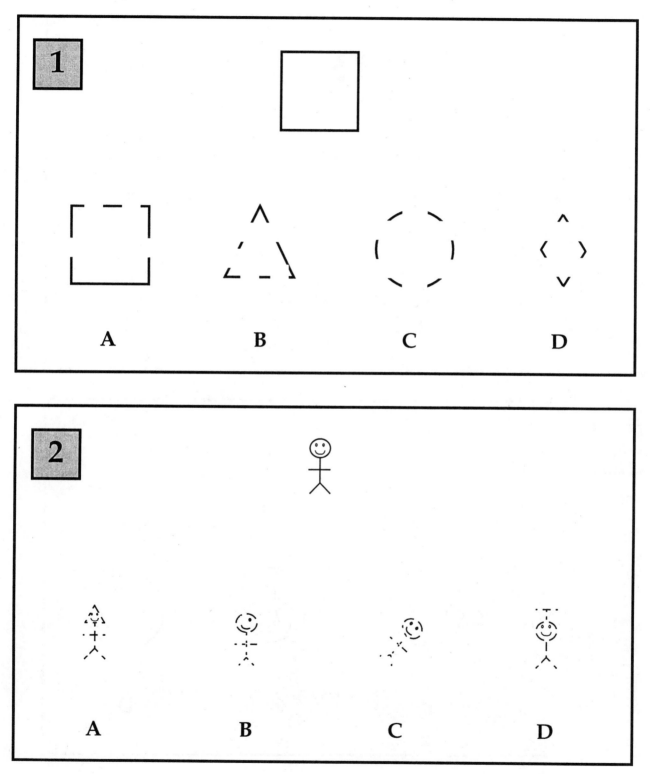

FINDING THE MATCHING SHAPE

DIRECTIONS: Match the incomplete form in the bottom row to its completed form in the top row.

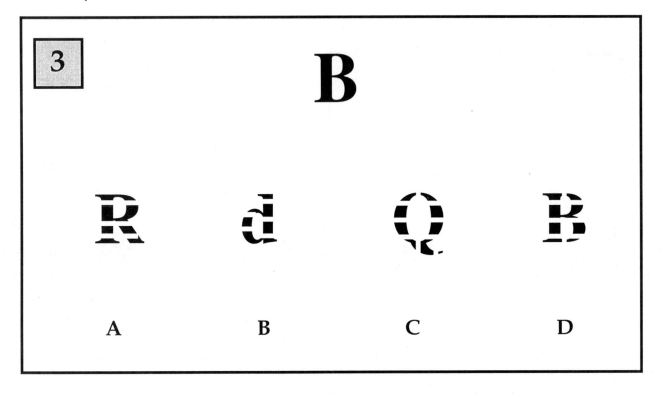

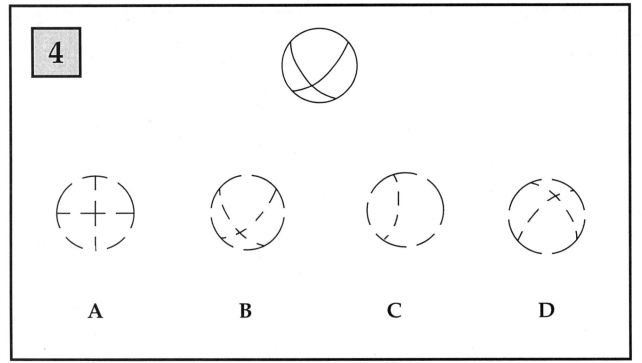

FINDING THE MATCHING SHAPE

DIRECTIONS: Match the incomplete form in the bottom row to its completed form in the top row.

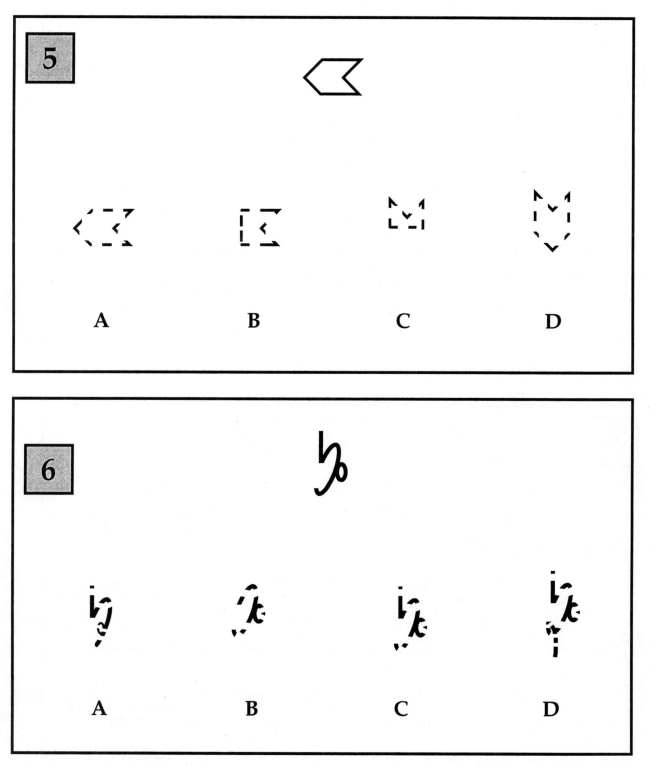

FINDING THE MATCHING SHAPE

DIRECTIONS: Match the incomplete form in the bottom row to its completed form in the top row.

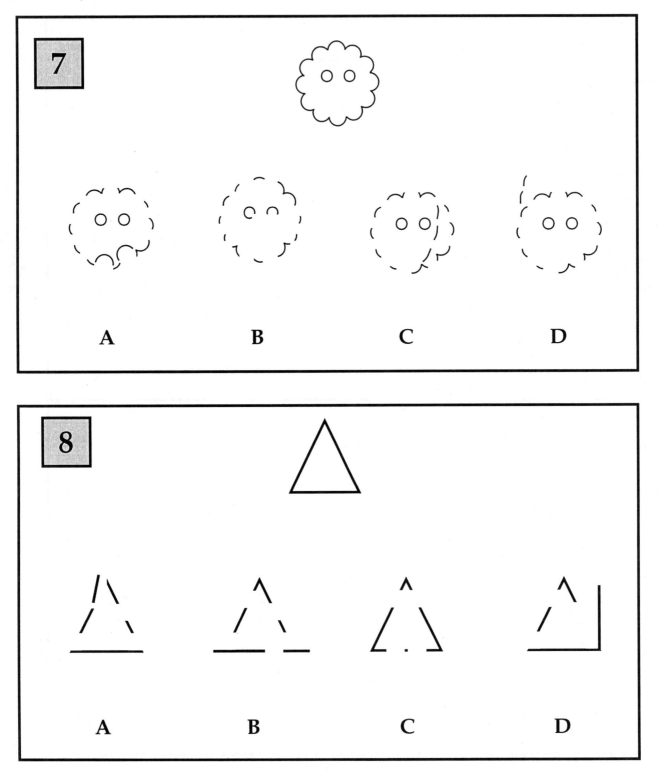

FINDING THE MATCHING SHAPE

DIRECTIONS: Match the incomplete form in the bottom row to its completed form in the top row.

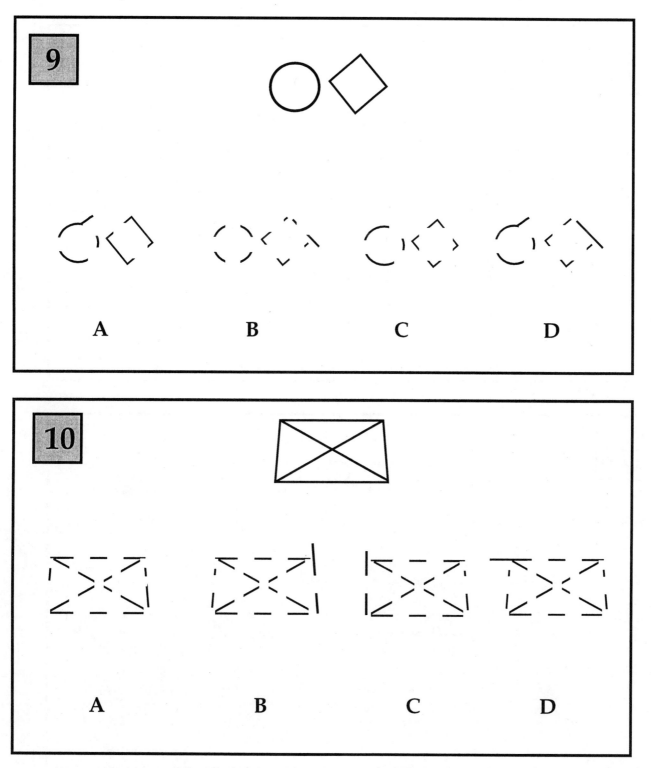

FINDING THE MATCHING SHAPE

DIRECTIONS: Match the incomplete form in the bottom row to its completed form in the top row.

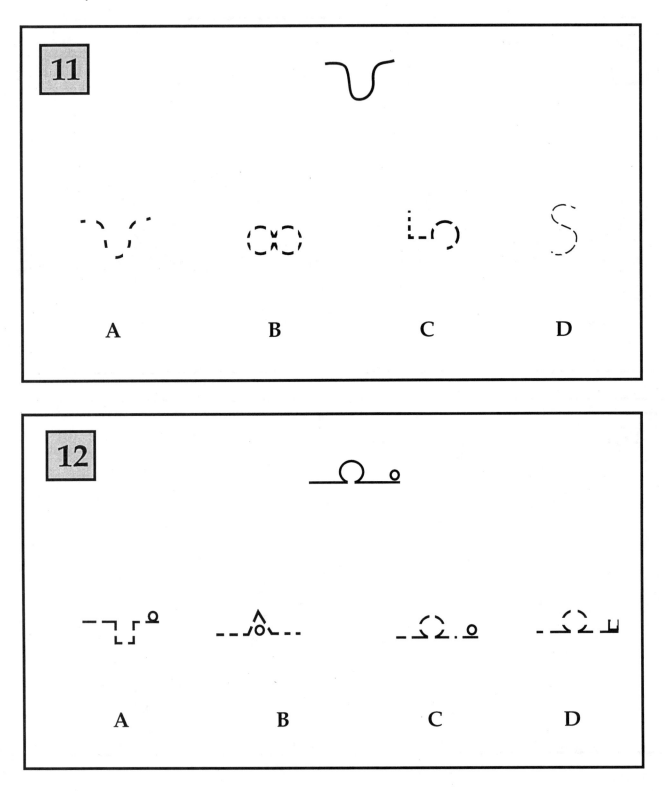

FINDING THE MATCHING SHAPE

DIRECTIONS: Match the incomplete form in the bottom row to its completed form in the top row.

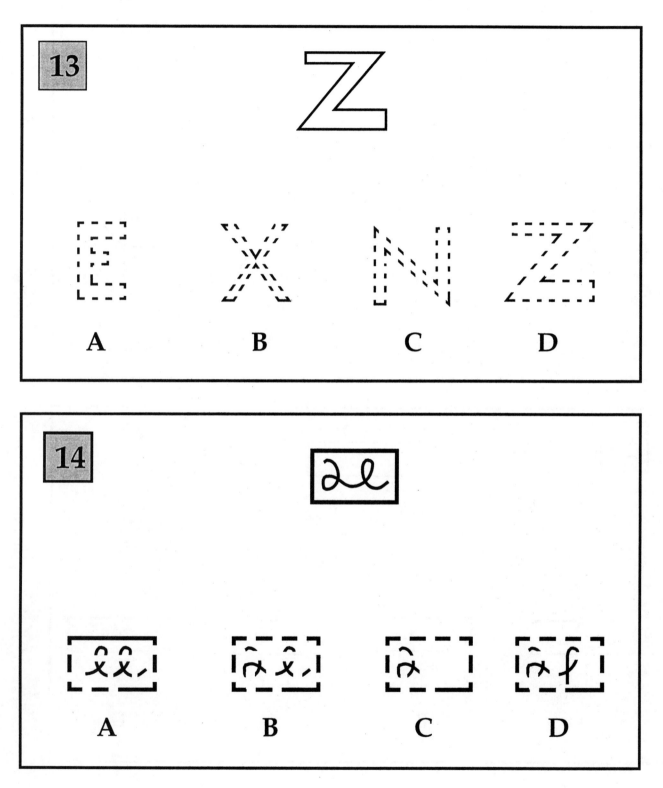

FINDING THE MATCHING SHAPE

DIRECTIONS: Match the incomplete form in the bottom row to its completed form in the top row.

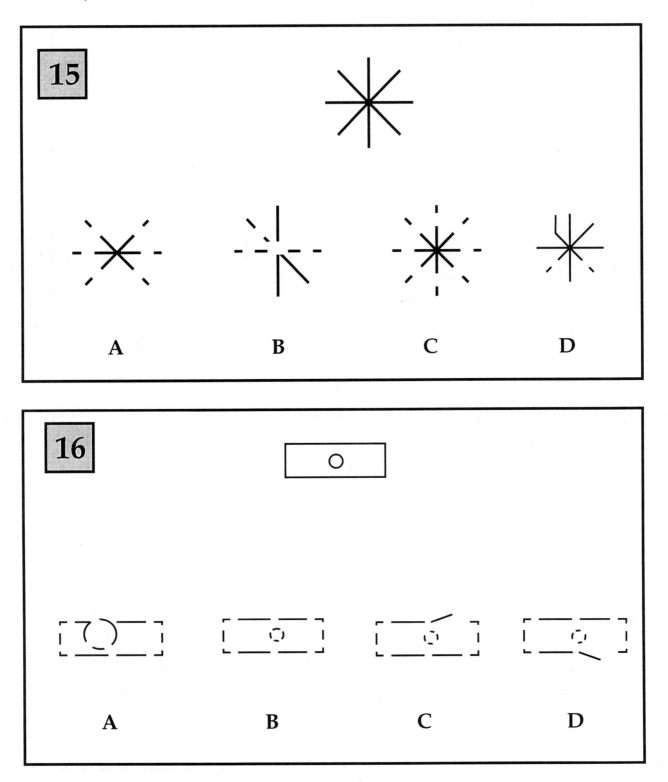

FINDING THE MATCHING SHAPE

DIRECTIONS: Match the incomplete form in the bottom row to its completed form in the top row.

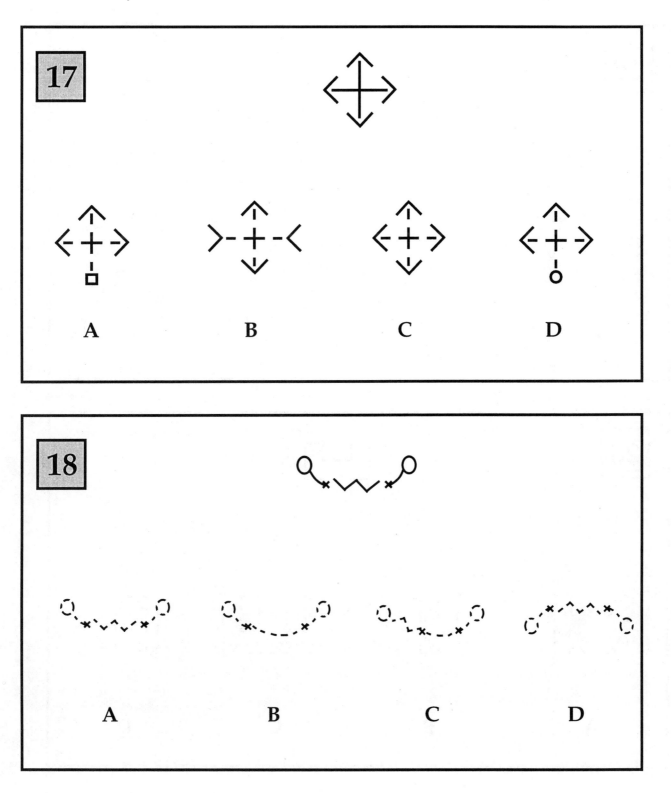

FINDING THE MATCHING SHAPE

DIRECTIONS: Match the incomplete form in the bottom row to its completed form in the top row.

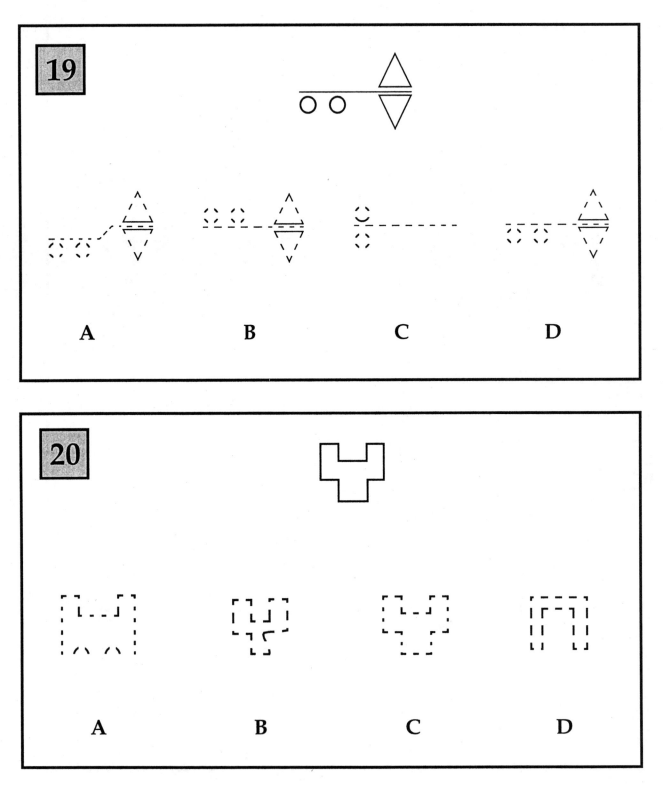

VISUAL FIGURE GROUND PRETEST

DIRECTIONS: Match the figure in the top row to one of the figures in the bottom row. Look closely — the matching figure may be hiding.

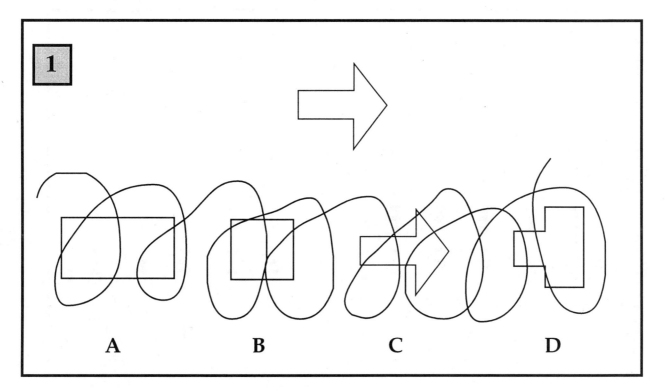

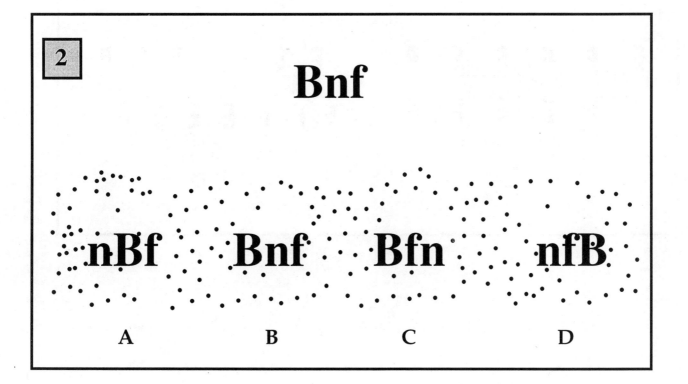

VISUAL FIGURE GROUND PRETEST

DIRECTIONS: Match the figure in the top row to one of the figures in the bottom row. Look closely — the matching figure may be hiding.

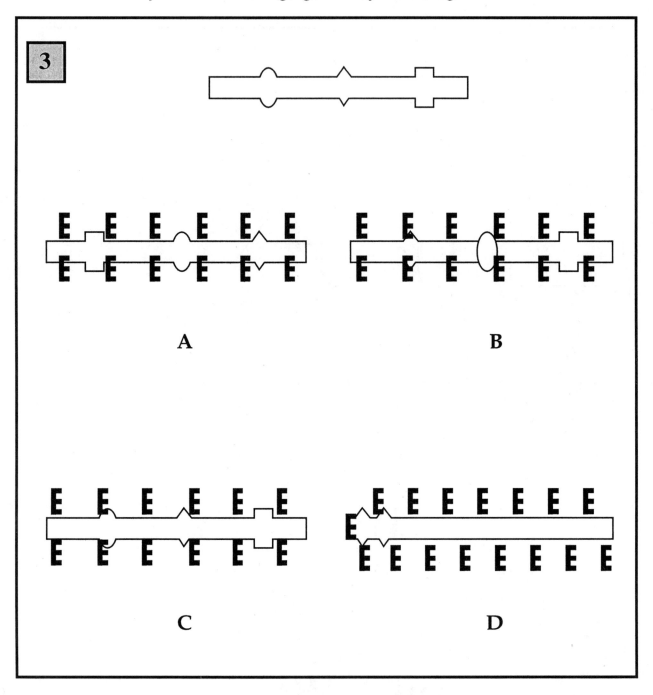

VISUAL FIGURE GROUND POSTTEST

DIRECTIONS: Match the figure in the top row to one of the figures in the bottom row. Look closely — the matching figure may be hiding.

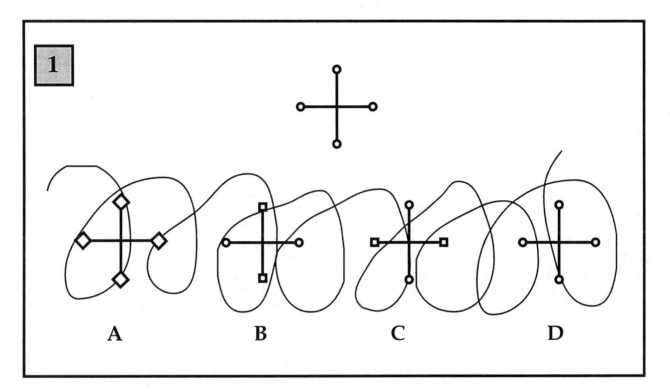

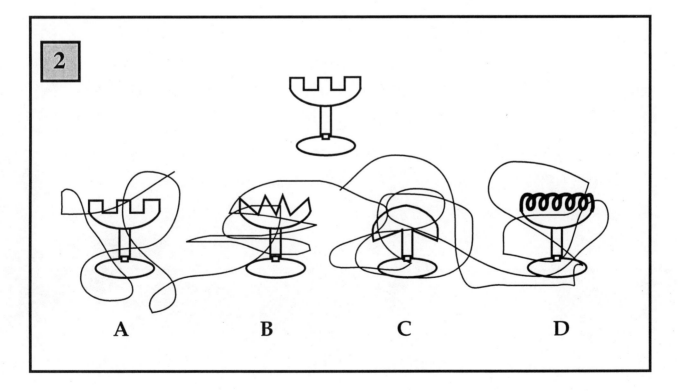

VISUAL FIGURE GROUND POSTTEST

DIRECTIONS: Match the figure in the top row to one of the figures in the bottom row. Look closely — the matching figure may be hiding.

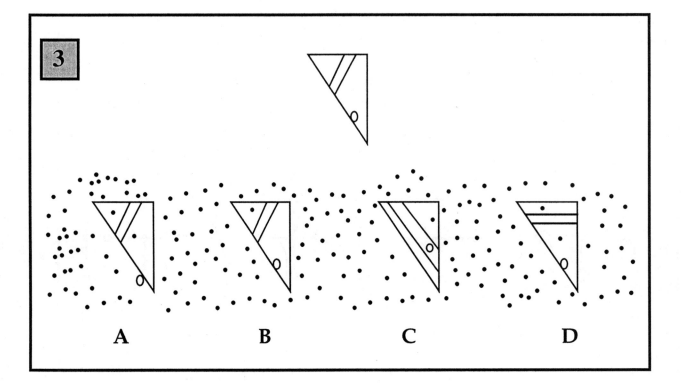

FINDING THE MATCHING FIGURE

DIRECTIONS: Match the figure in the top row to one of the figures in the bottom row. Look closely—the matching figure may be hiding.

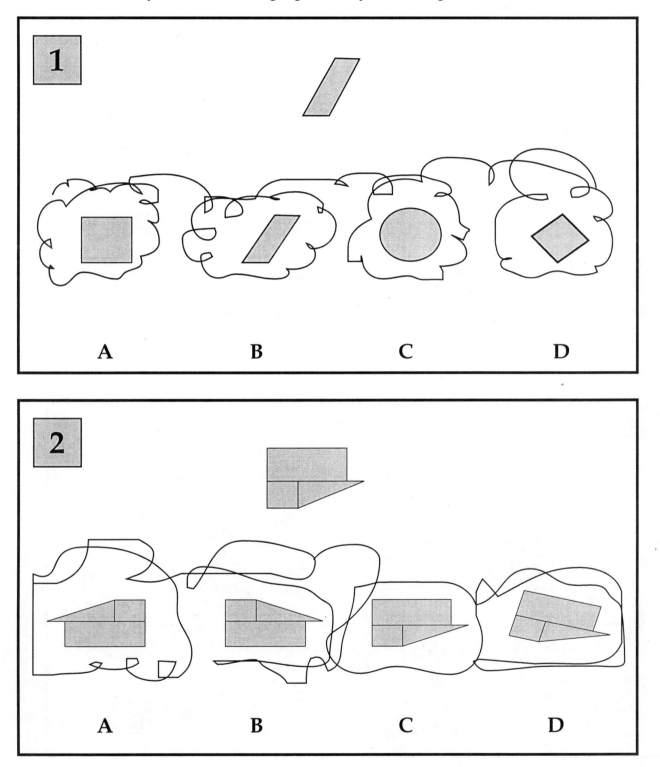

FINDING THE MATCHING FIGURE

DIRECTIONS: Match the figure in the top row to one of the figures in the bottom row. Look closely—the matching figure may be hiding.

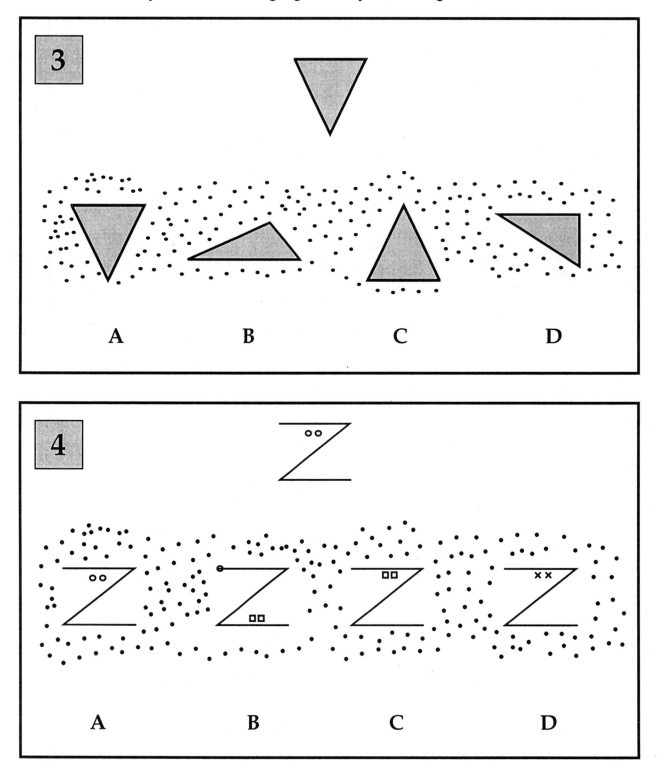

FINDING THE MATCHING FIGURE

DIRECTIONS: Match the figure in the top row to one of the figures in the bottom row. Look closely—the matching figure may be hiding.

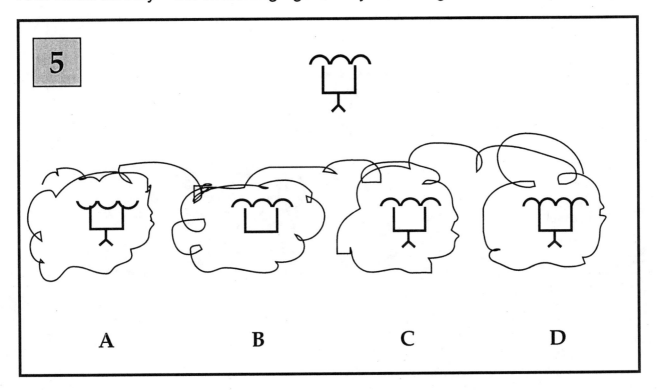

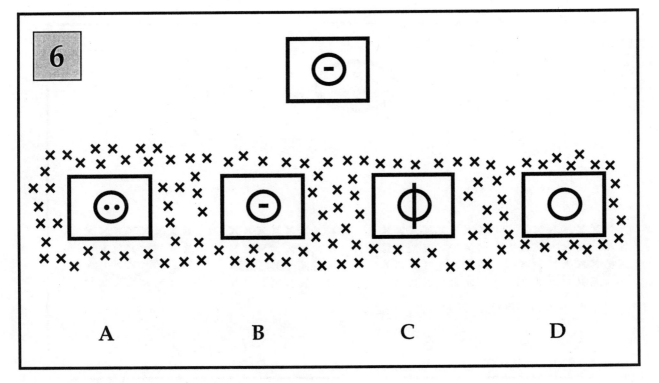

FINDING THE MATCHING FIGURE

DIRECTIONS: Match the figure in the top row to one of the figures in the bottom row. Look closely—the matching figure may be hiding.

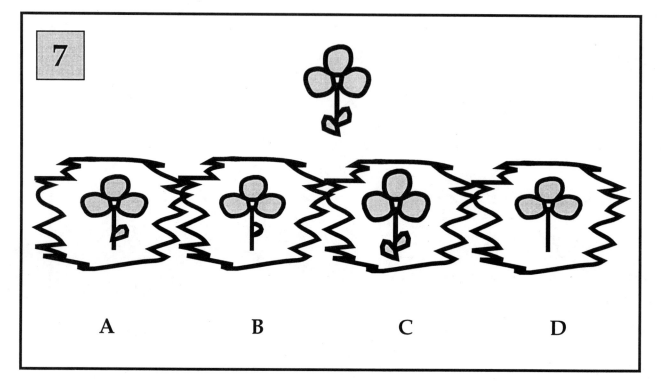

FINDING THE MATCHING FIGURE

DIRECTIONS: Match the figure in the top row to one of the figures in the bottom row. Look closely—the matching figure may be hiding.

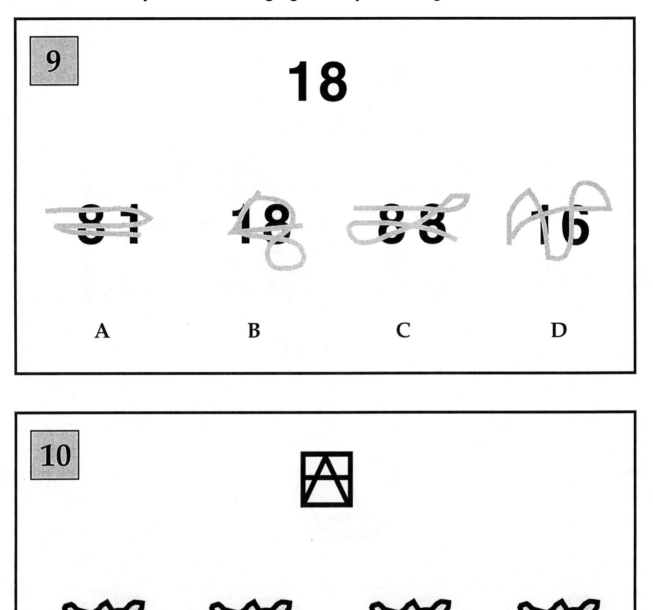

FINDING THE MATCHING FIGURE

DIRECTIONS: Match the figure in the top row to one of the figures in the bottom row. Look closely—the matching figure may be hiding.

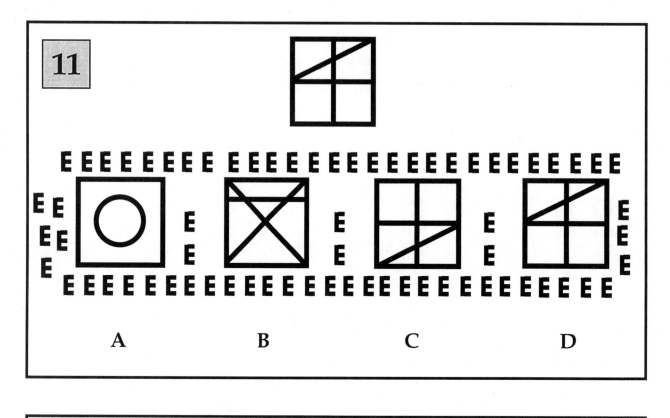

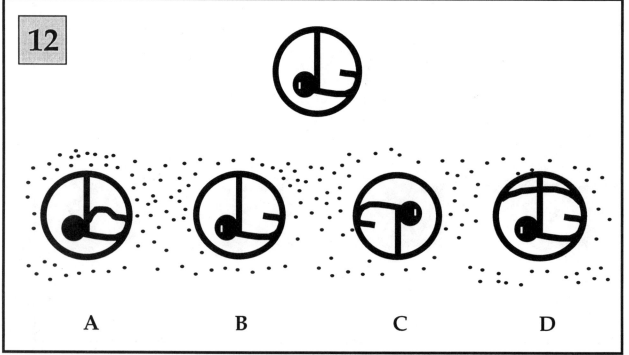

FINDING THE MATCHING FIGURE

DIRECTIONS: Match the figure in the top row to one of the figures in the bottom row. Look closely—the matching figure may be hiding.

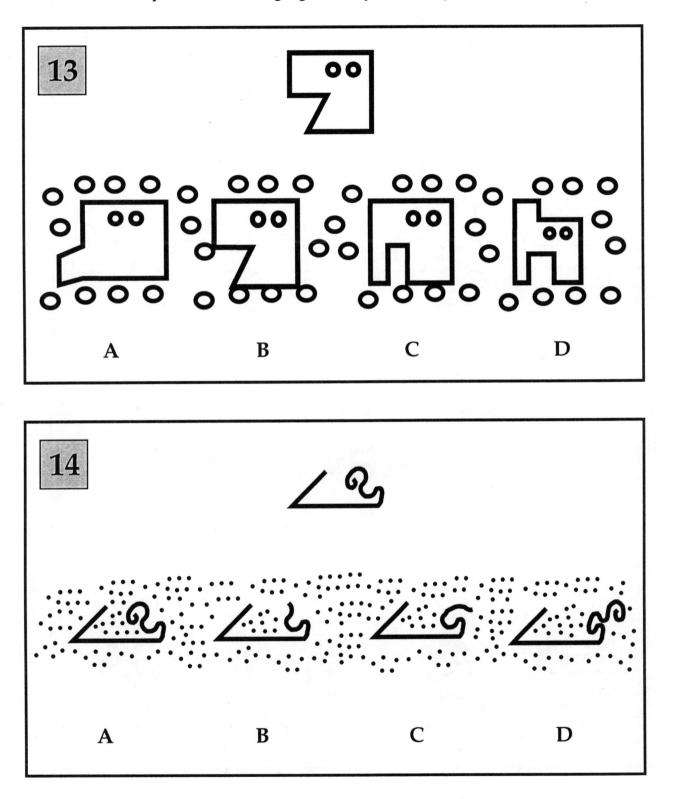

FINDING THE MATCHING FIGURE

DIRECTIONS: Match the figure in the top row to one of the figures in the bottom row. Look closely—the matching figure may be hiding.

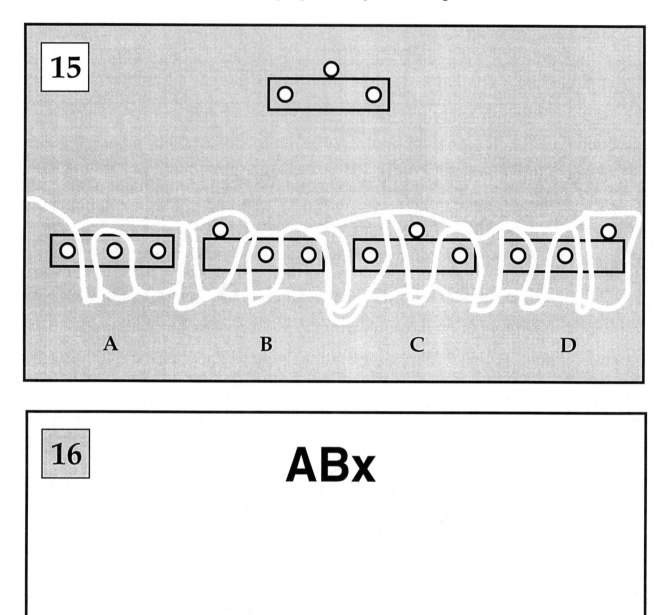

FINDING THE MATCHING FIGURE

DIRECTIONS: Match the figure in the top row to one of the figures in the bottom row. Look closely—the matching figure may be hiding.

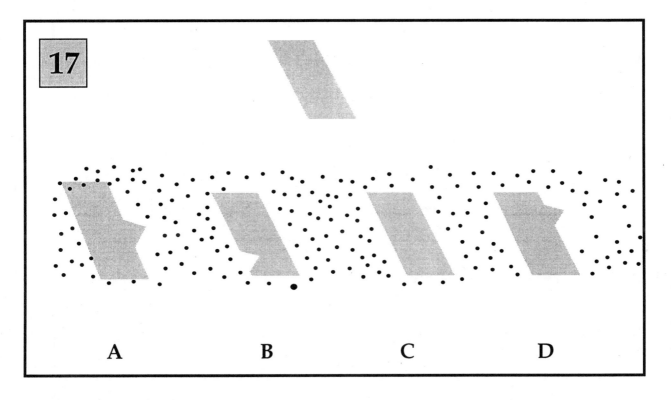

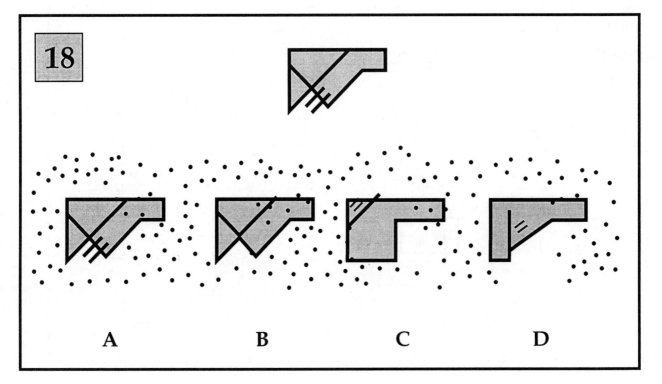

FINDING THE MATCHING FIGURE

DIRECTIONS: Match the figure in the top row to one of the figures in the bottom row. Look closely—the matching figure may be hiding.

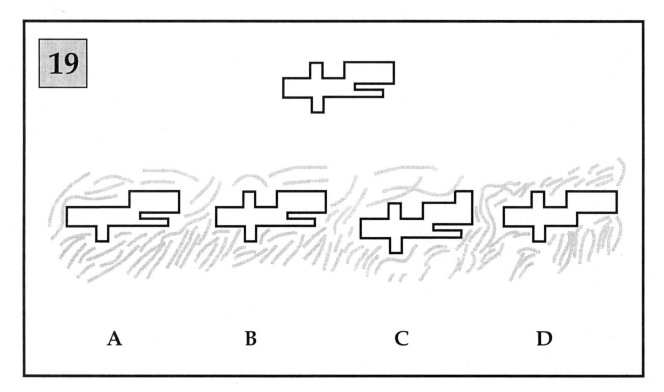

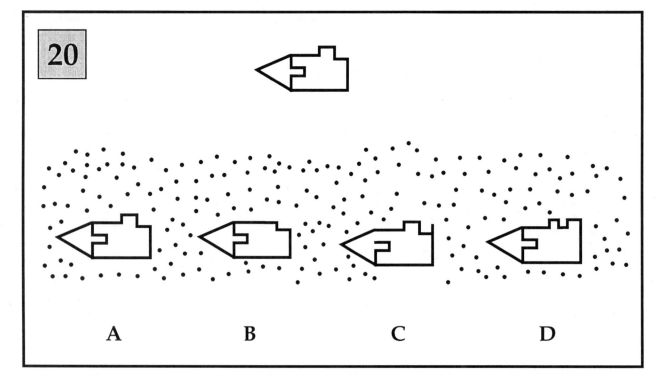

VISUAL FORM CONSTANCY PRETEST

DIRECTIONS: Match the top figure to one of the bottom figures. The matching figure might be bigger, smaller, darker, turned on its side, flipped, or upside down.

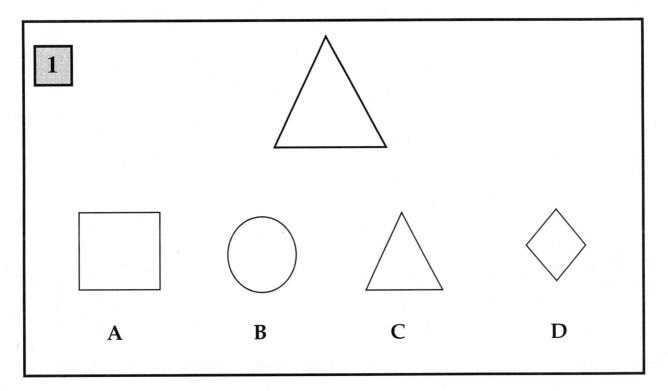

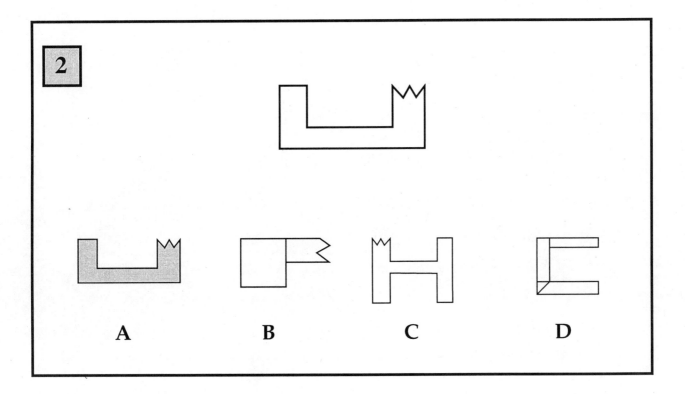

VISUAL FORM CONSTANCY PRETEST

DIRECTIONS: Match the top figure to one of the bottom figures. The matching figure might be bigger, smaller, darker, turned on its side, flipped, or upside down.

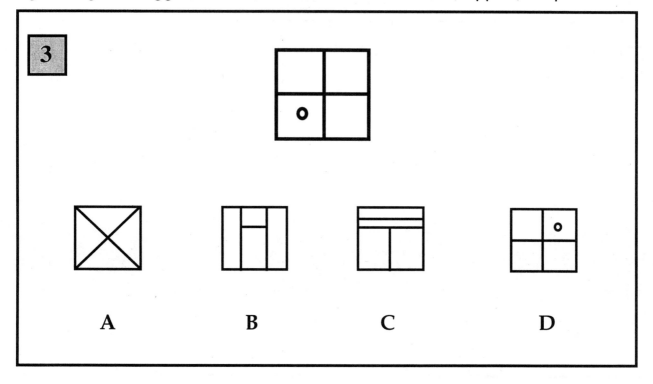

VISUAL FORM CONSTANCY POSTTEST

DIRECTIONS: Match the top figure to one of the bottom figures. The matching figure might be bigger, smaller, darker, turned on its side, flipped, or upside down.

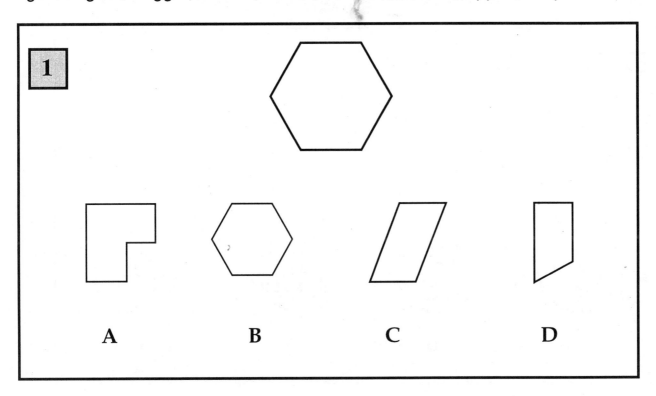

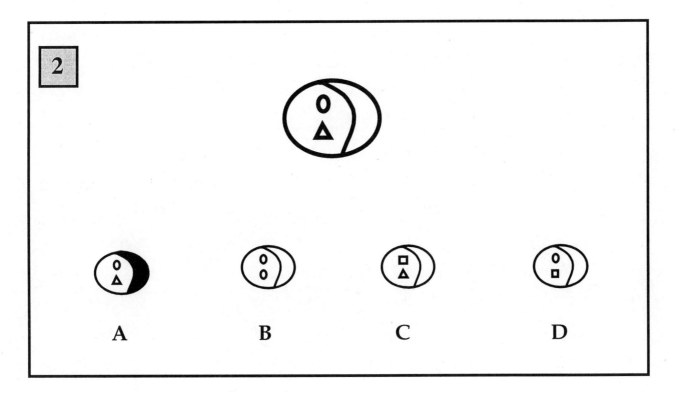

VISUAL FORM CONSTANCY POSTTEST

DIRECTIONS: Match the top figure to one of the bottom figures. The matching figure might be bigger, smaller, darker, turned on its side, flipped, or upside down.

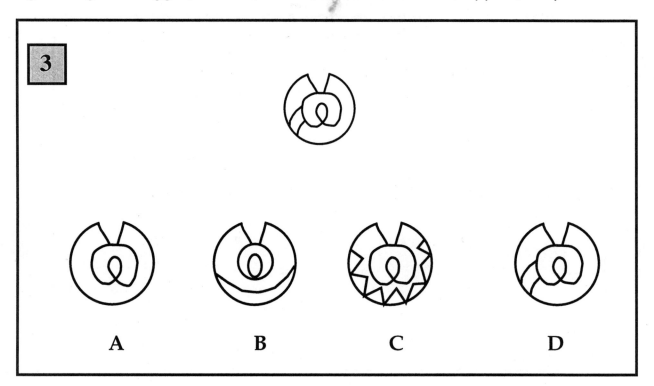

FINDING THE CORRECT FIGURE

DIRECTIONS: Match the top figure to one of the bottom figures. The matching figure might be bigger, smaller, darker, turned on its side, flipped, or upside down.

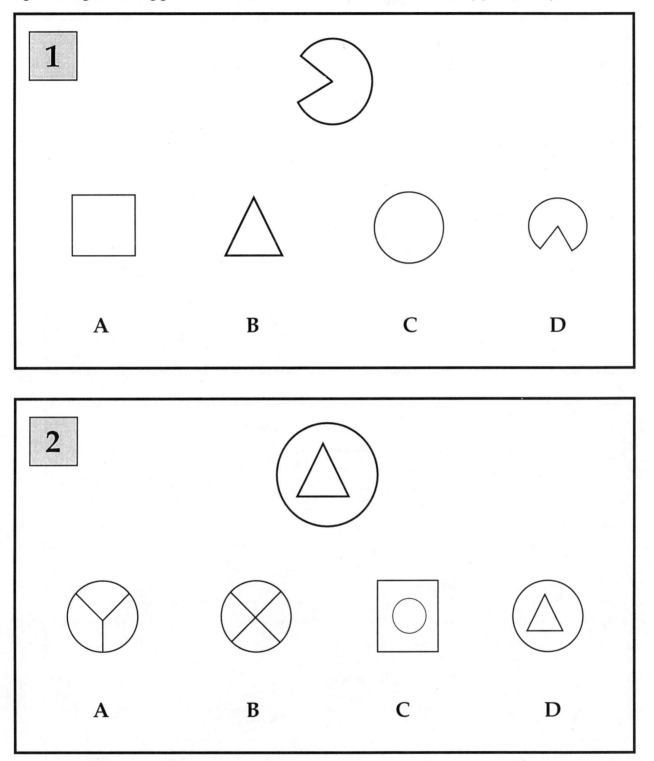

FINDING THE CORRECT FIGURE

DIRECTIONS: Match the top figure to one of the bottom figures. The matching figure might be bigger, smaller, darker, turned on its side, flipped, or upside down.

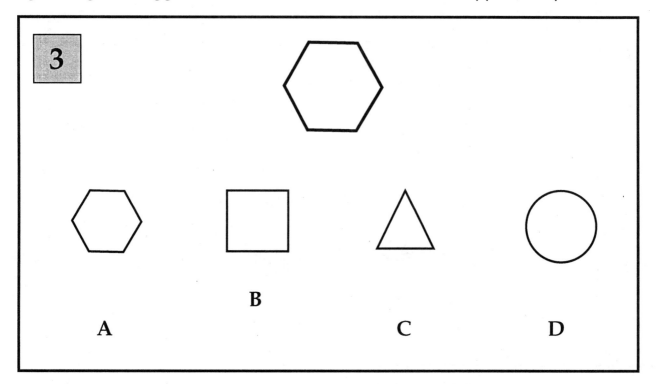

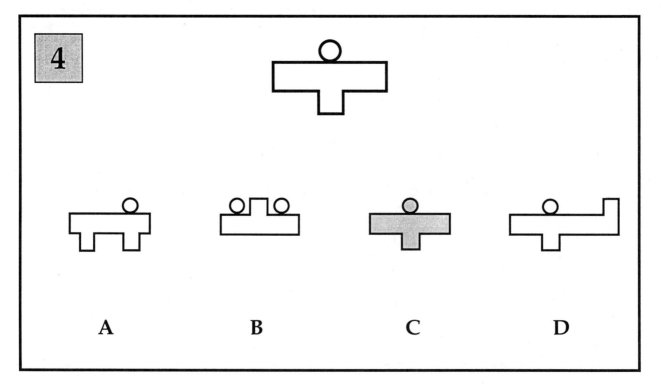

FINDING THE CORRECT FIGURE

DIRECTIONS: Match the top figure to one of the bottom figures. The matching figure might be bigger, smaller, darker, turned on its side, flipped, or upside down.

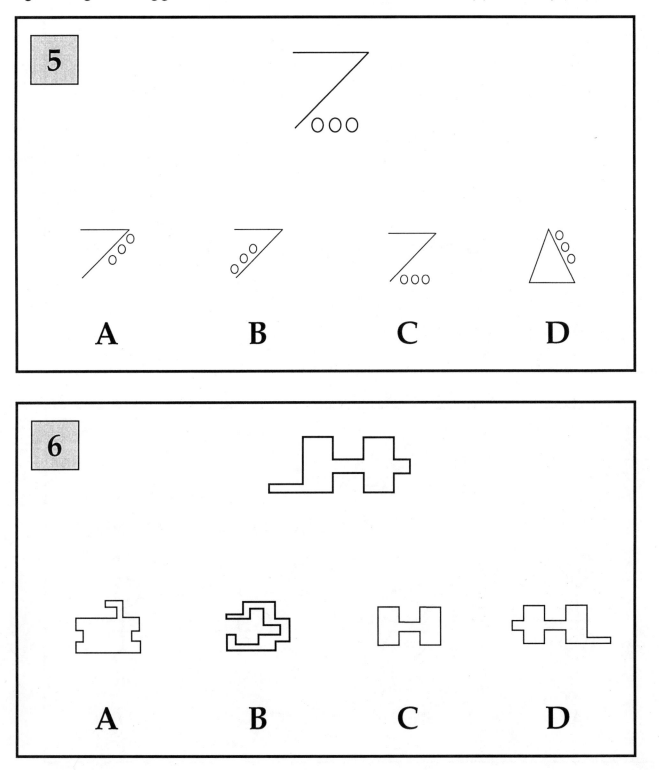

FINDING THE CORRECT FIGURE

DIRECTIONS: Match the top figure to one of the bottom figures. The matching figure might be bigger, smaller, darker, turned on its side, flipped, or upside down.

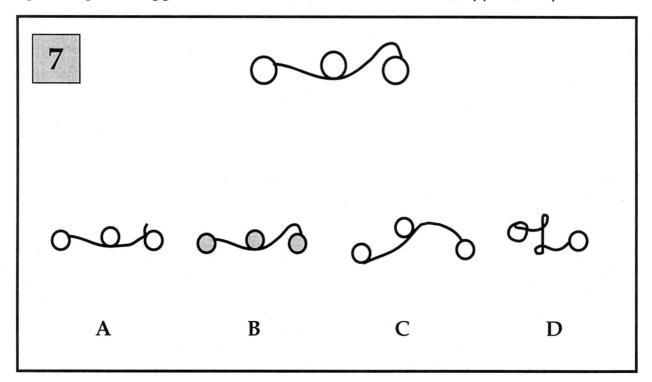

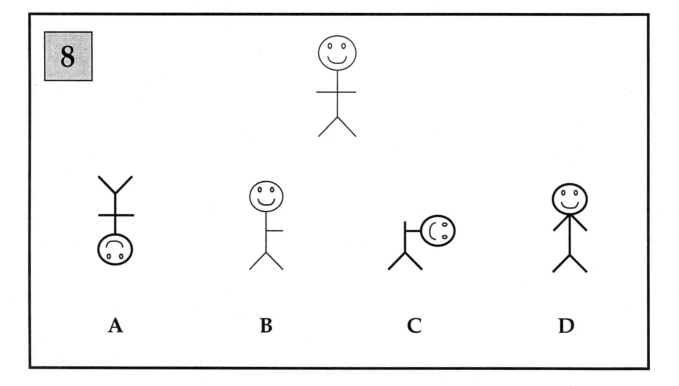

FINDING THE CORRECT FIGURE

DIRECTIONS: Match the top figure to one of the bottom figures. The matching figure might be bigger, smaller, darker, turned on its side, flipped, or upside down.

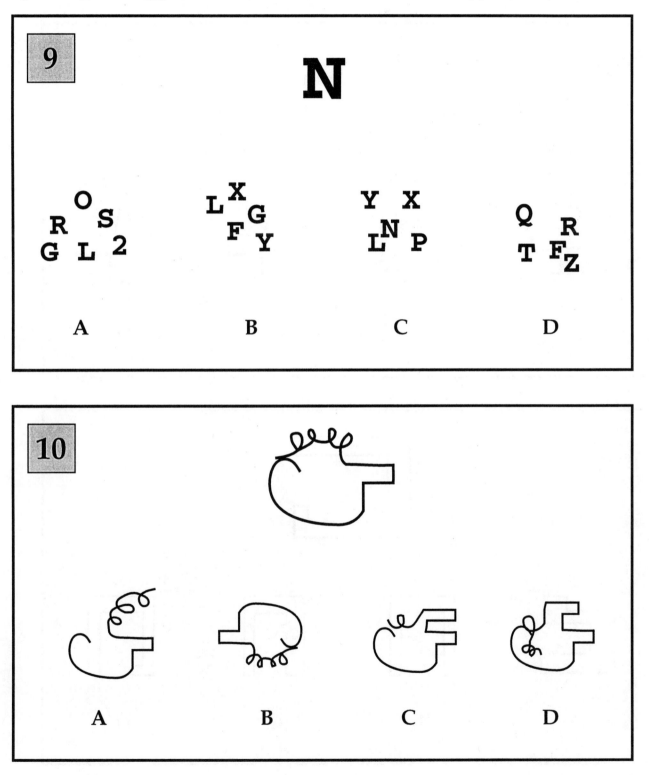

FINDING THE CORRECT FIGURE

DIRECTIONS: Match the top figure to one of the bottom figures. The matching figure might be bigger, smaller, darker, turned on its side, flipped, or upside down.

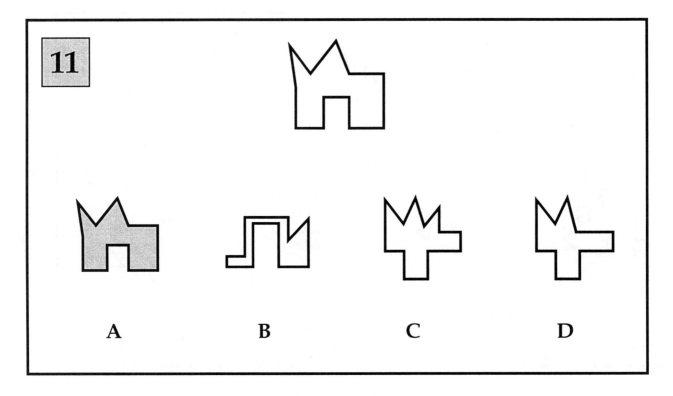

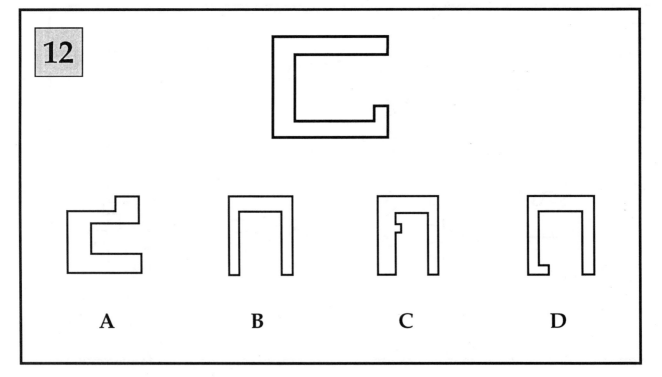

FINDING THE CORRECT FIGURE

DIRECTIONS: Match the top figure to one of the bottom figures. The matching figure might be bigger, smaller, darker, turned on its side, flipped, or upside down.

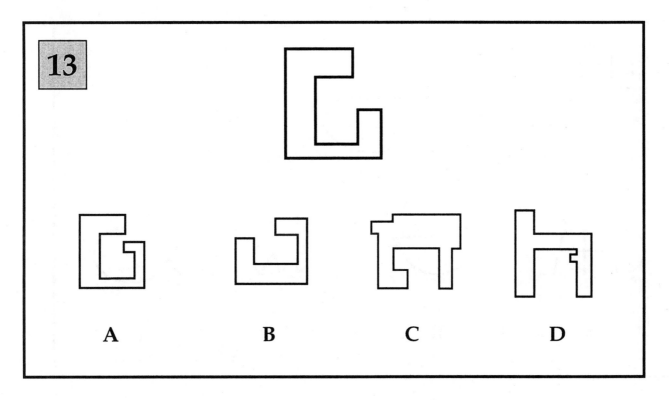

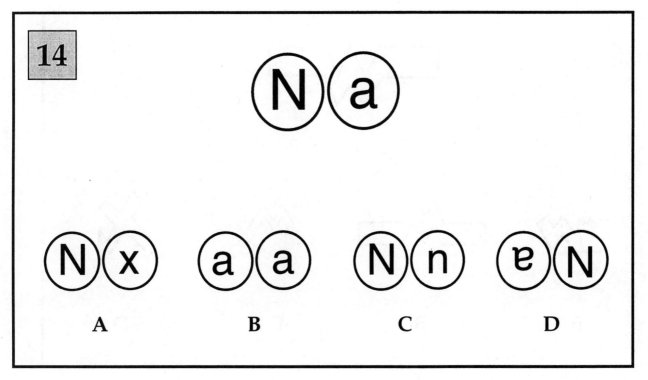

FINDING THE CORRECT FIGURE

DIRECTIONS: Match the top figure to one of the bottom figures. The matching figure might be bigger, smaller, darker, turned on its side, flipped, or upside down.

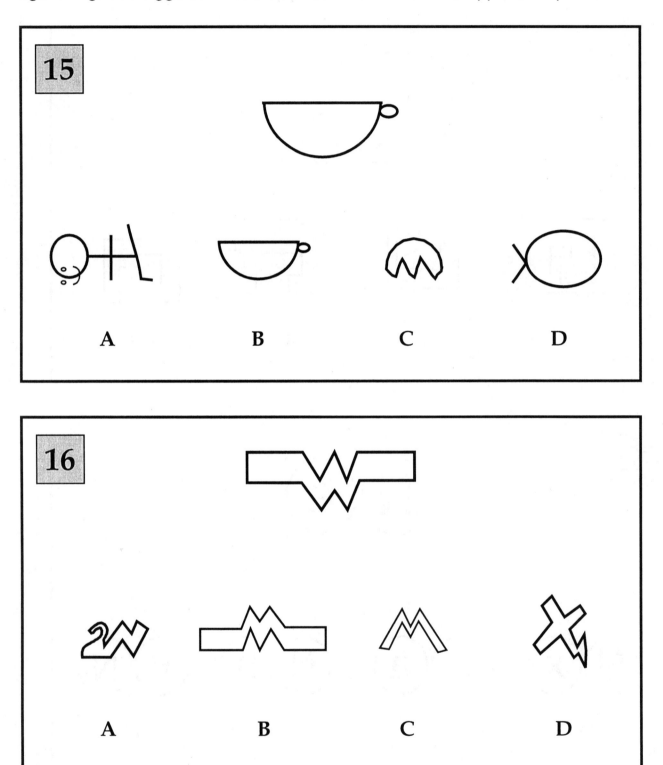

FINDING THE CORRECT FIGURE

DIRECTIONS: Match the top figure to one of the bottom figures. The matching figure might be bigger, smaller, darker, turned on its side, flipped, or upside down.

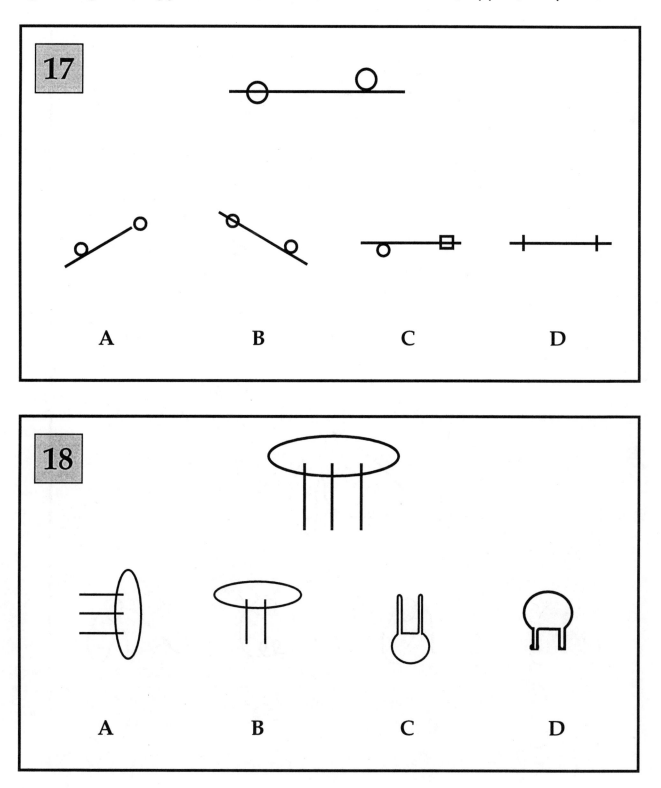

FINDING THE CORRECT FIGURE

DIRECTIONS: Match the top figure to one of the bottom figures. The matching figure might be bigger, smaller, darker, turned on its side, flipped, or upside down.

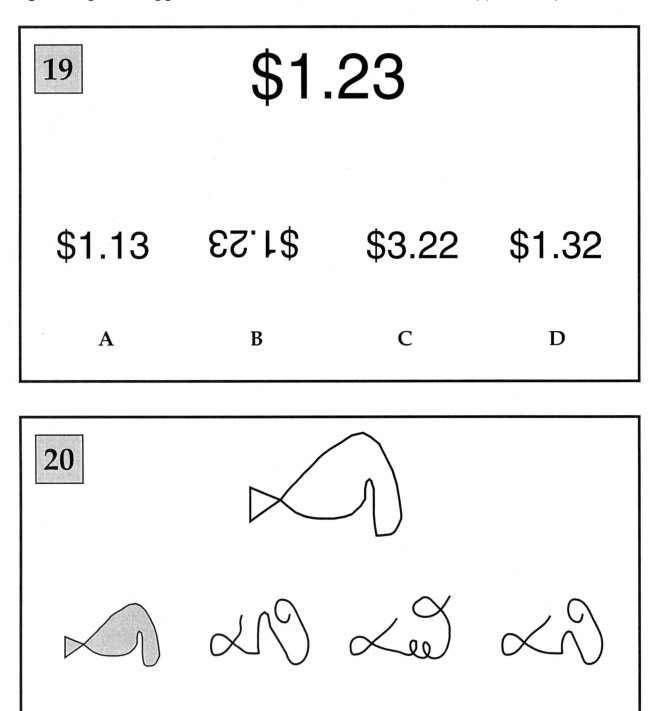

VISUAL MEMORY PRETEST

DIRECTIONS: Look at the figure on this page. Then turn the page and find the matching figure. Do not look back at this page.

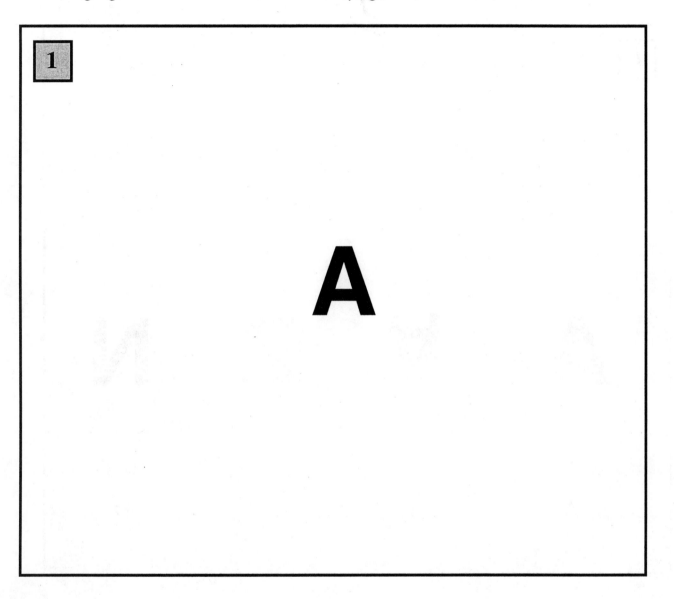

VISUAL MEMORY PRETEST

DIRECTIONS: Match one of the figures on this page to the figure on the page before. Do not look back at the page before.

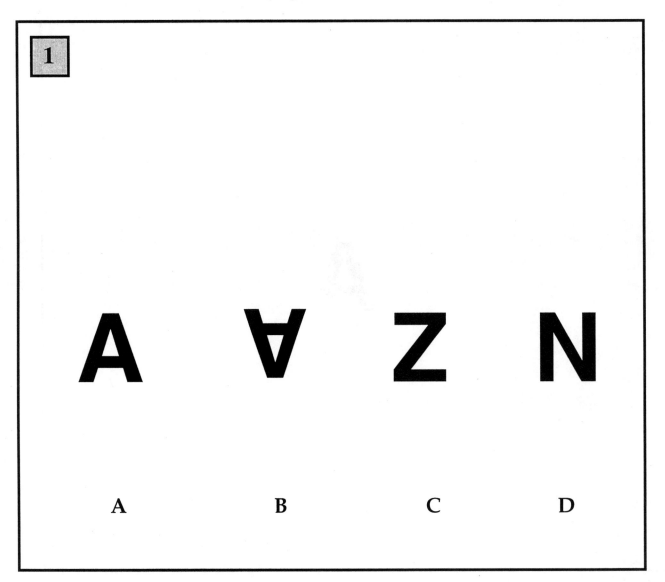

© 1998 CRITICAL THINKING BOOKS & SOFTWARE • WWW.CRITICALTHINKING.COM • 800-458-4849

VISUAL MEMORY PRETEST

DIRECTIONS: Look at the figure on this page. Then turn the page and find the matching figure. Do not look back at this page.

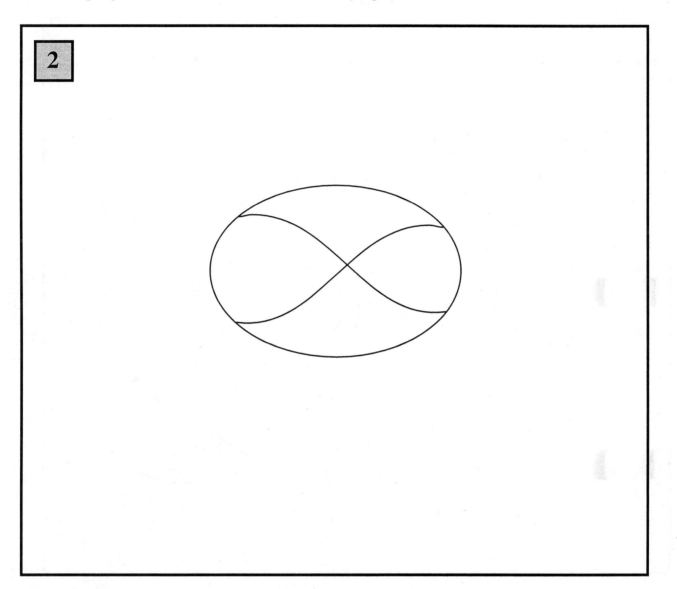

VISUAL MEMORY PRETEST

DIRECTIONS: Match one of the figures on this page to the figure on the page before. Do not look back at the page before.

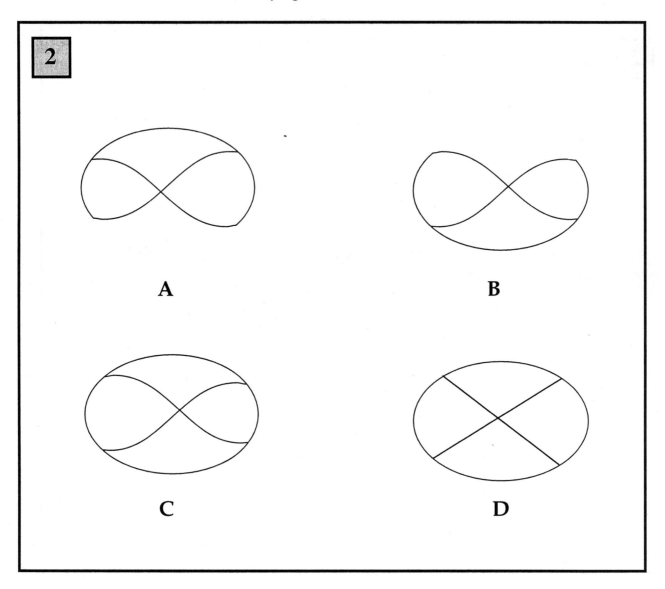

2

A

B

C

D

VISUAL MEMORY PRETEST

DIRECTIONS: Look at the figure on this page. Then turn the page and find the matching figure. Do not look back at this page.

VISUAL MEMORY PRETEST

DIRECTIONS: Match one of the figures on this page to the figure on the page before. Do not look back at the page before.

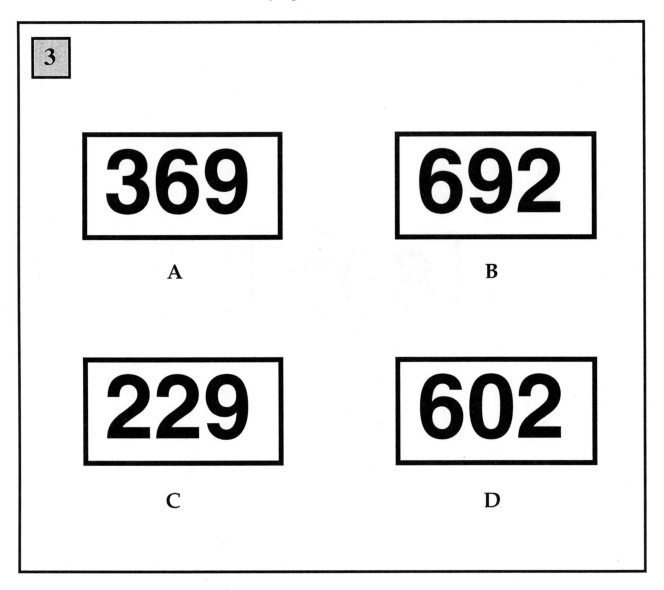

VISUAL MEMORY POSTTEST

DIRECTIONS: Look at the figure on this page. Then turn the page and find the matching figure. Do not look back at this page.

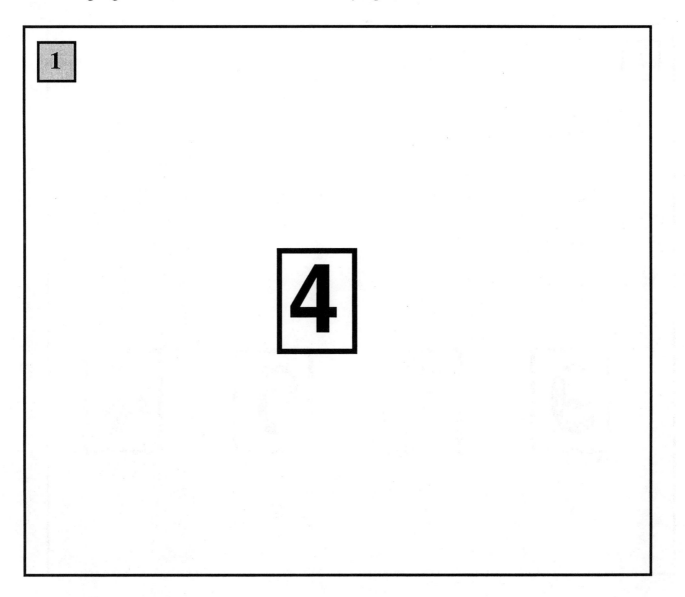

VISUAL MEMORY POSTTEST

DIRECTIONS: Match one of the figures on this page to the figure on the page before. Do not look back at the page before.

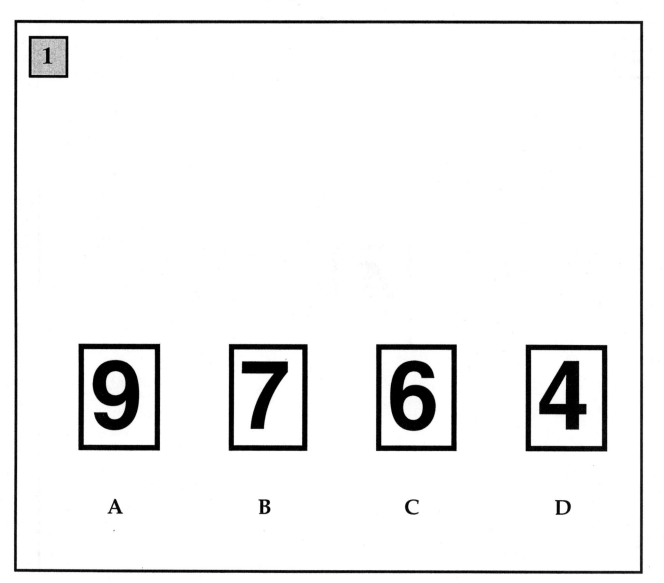

VISUAL MEMORY POSTTEST

DIRECTIONS: Look at the figure on this page. Then turn the page and find the matching figure. Do not look back at this page.

VISUAL MEMORY POSTTEST

DIRECTIONS: Match one of the figures on this page to the figure on the page before. Do not look back at the page before.

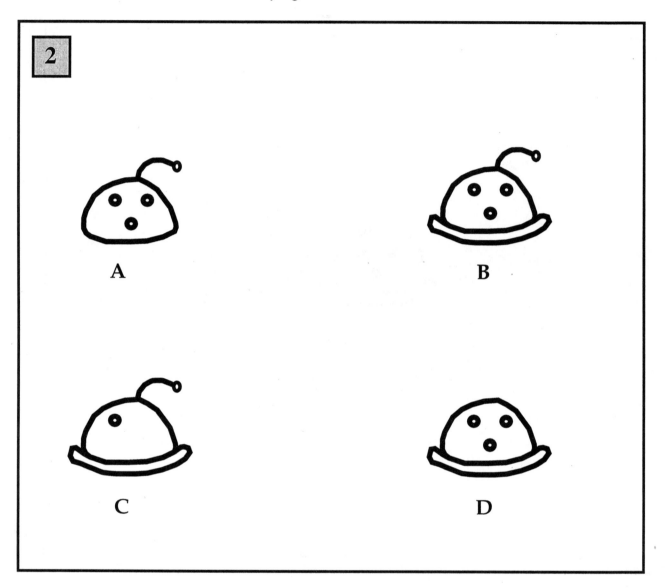

VISUAL MEMORY POSTTEST

DIRECTIONS: Look at the figure on this page. Then turn the page and find the matching figure. Do not look back at this page.

VISUAL MEMORY POSTTEST

DIRECTIONS: Match one of the figures on this page to the figure on the page before. Do not look back at the page before.

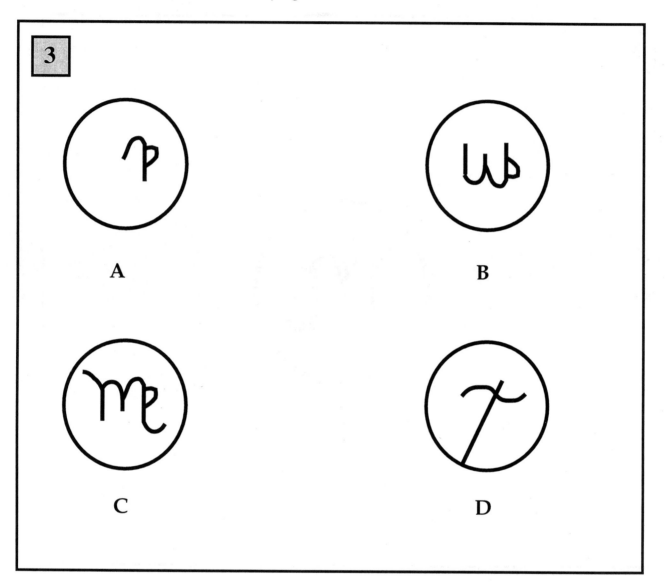

FINDING THE MATCHING FIGURE

DIRECTIONS: Look at the figure on this page. Then turn the page and find the matching figure. Do not look back at this page.

FINDING THE MATCHING FIGURE

DIRECTIONS: Find the figure on this page that matches the figure on the page before. Do not look back at the page before.

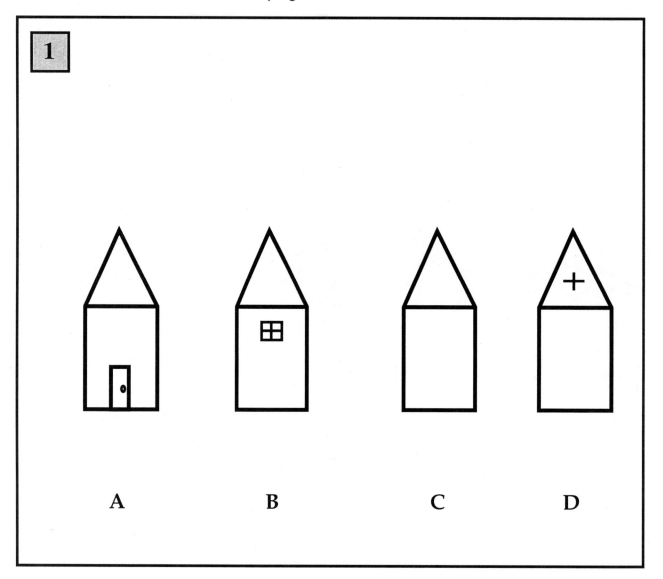

FINDING THE MATCHING FIGURE

DIRECTIONS: Look at the figure on this page. Then turn the page and find the matching figure. Do not look back at this page.

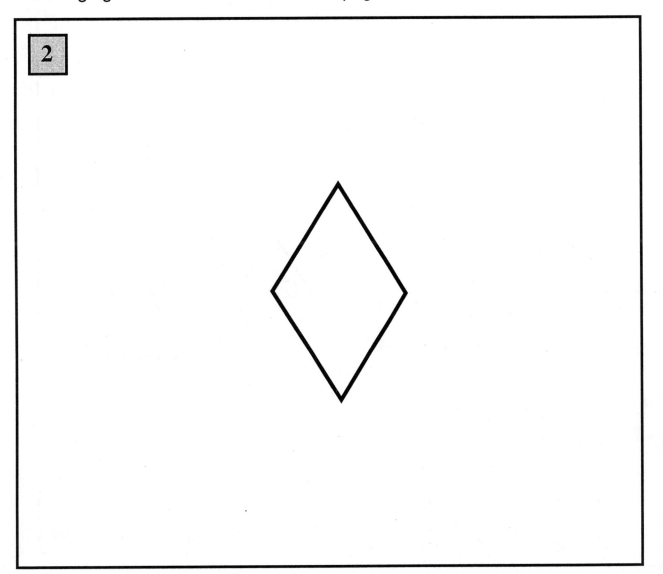

FINDING THE MATCHING FIGURE

DIRECTIONS: Find the figure on this page that matches the figure on the page before. Do not look back at the page before.

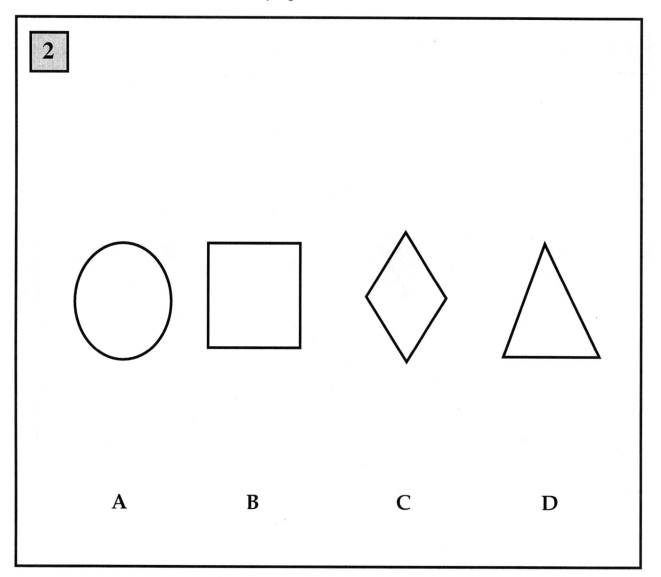

FINDING THE MATCHING FIGURE

DIRECTIONS: Look at the figure on this page. Then turn the page and find the matching figure. Do not look back at this page.

FINDING THE MATCHING FIGURE

DIRECTIONS: Find the figure on this page that matches the figure on the page before. Do not look back at the page before.

FINDING THE MATCHING FIGURE

DIRECTIONS: Look at the figure on this page. Then turn the page and find the matching figure. Do not look back at this page.

FINDING THE MATCHING FIGURE

DIRECTIONS: Find the figure on this page that matches the figure on the page before. Do not look back at the page before.

FINDING THE MATCHING FIGURE

DIRECTIONS: Look at the figure on this page. Then turn the page and find the matching figure. Do not look back at this page.

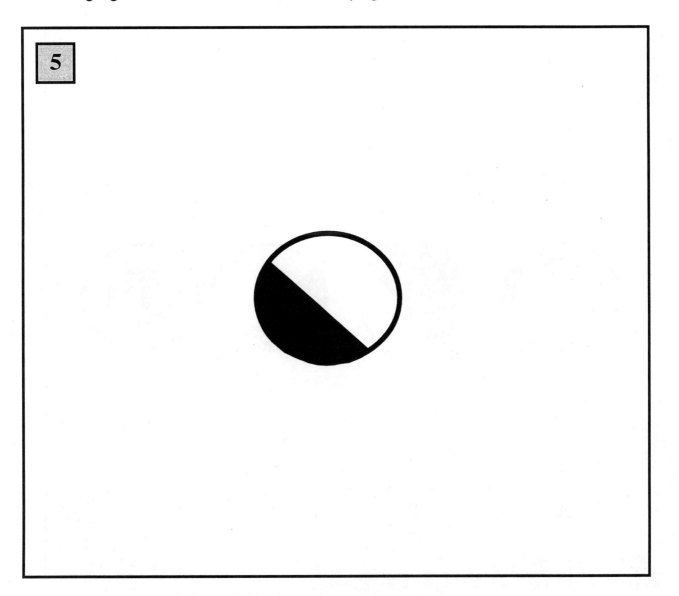

FINDING THE MATCHING FIGURE

DIRECTIONS: Find the figure on this page that matches the figure on the page before. Do not look back at the page before.

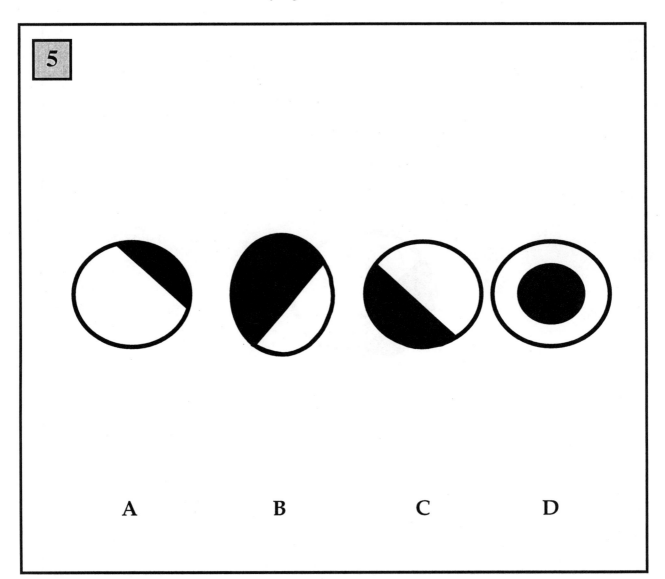

FINDING THE MATCHING FIGURE

DIRECTIONS: Look at the figure on this page. Then turn the page and find the matching figure. Do not look back at this page.

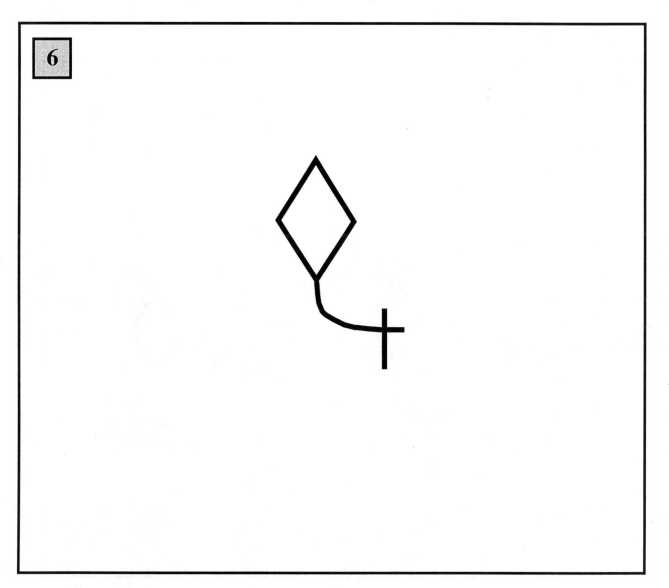

FINDING THE MATCHING FIGURE

DIRECTIONS: Find the figure on this page that matches the figure on the page before. Do not look back at the page before.

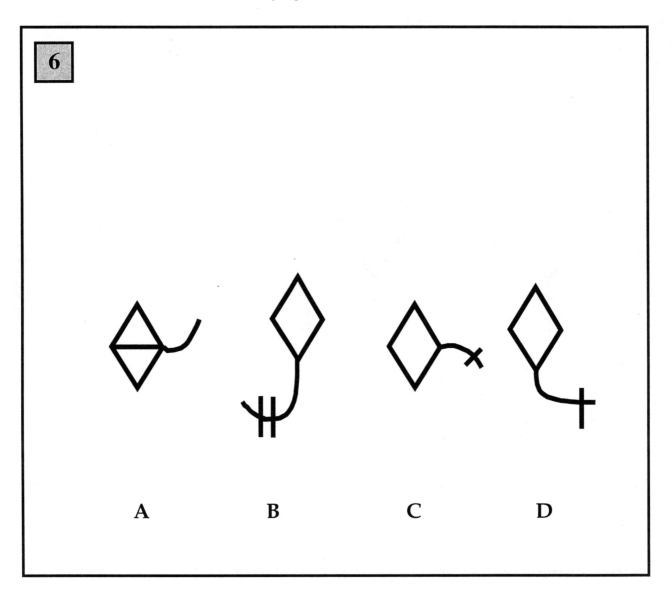

A   B   C   D

FINDING THE MATCHING FIGURE

DIRECTIONS: Look at the figure on this page. Then turn the page and find the matching figure. Do not look back at this page.

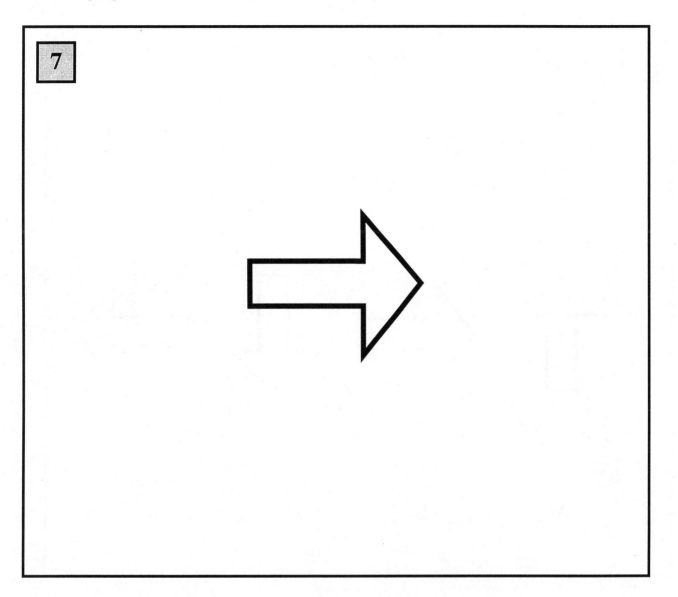

FINDING THE MATCHING FIGURE

DIRECTIONS: Find the figure on this page that matches the figure on the page before. Do not look back at the page before.

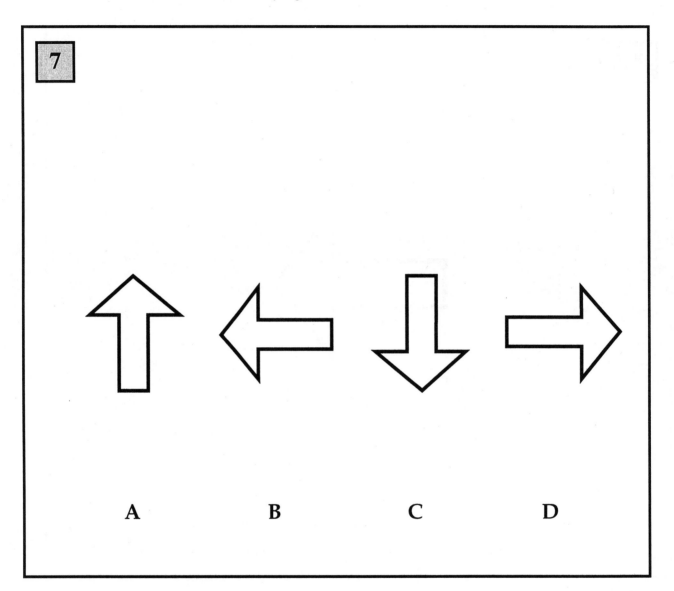

FINDING THE MATCHING FIGURE

DIRECTIONS: Look at the figure on this page. Then turn the page and find the matching figure. Do not look back at this page.

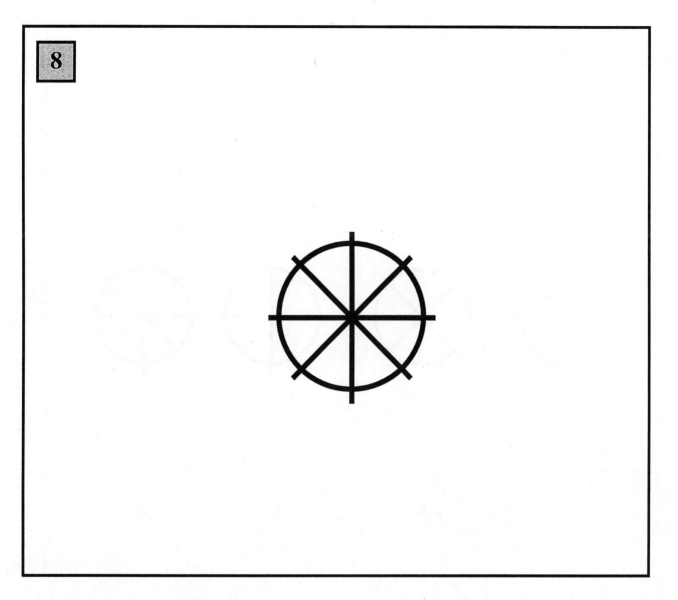

FINDING THE MATCHING FIGURE

DIRECTIONS: Find the figure on this page that matches the figure on the page before. Do not look back at the page before.

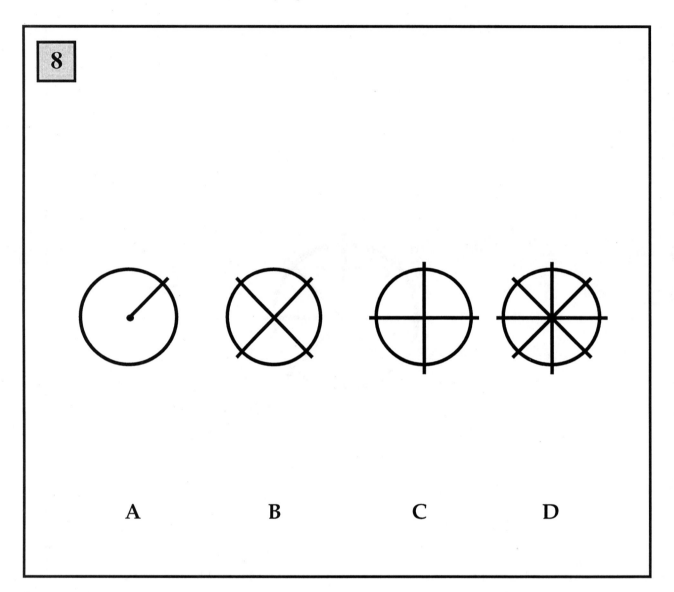

FINDING THE MATCHING FIGURE

DIRECTIONS: Look at the figure on this page. Then turn the page and find the matching figure. Do not look back at this page.

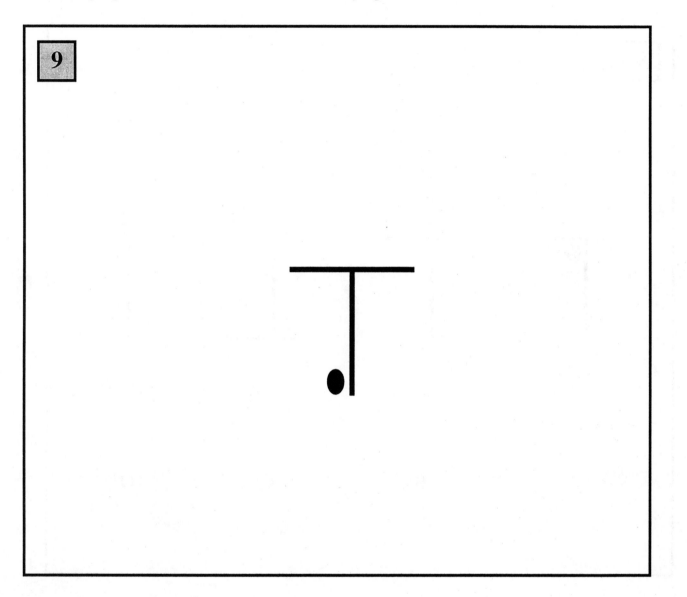

FINDING THE MATCHING FIGURE

DIRECTIONS: Find the figure on this page that matches the figure on the page before. Do not look back at the page before.

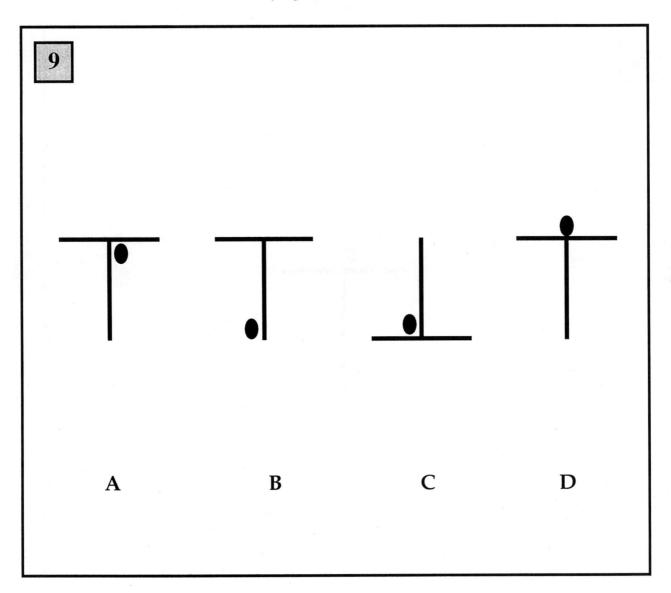

FINDING THE MATCHING FIGURE

DIRECTIONS: Look at the figure on this page. Then turn the page and find the matching figure. Do not look back at this page.

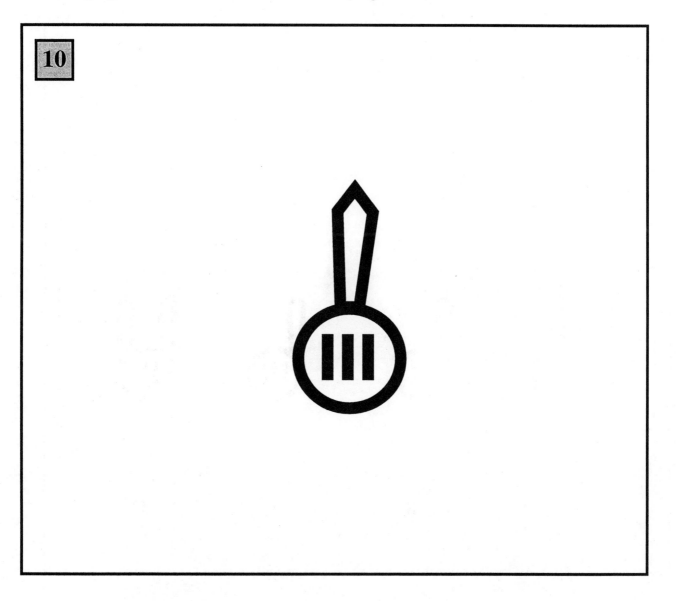

FINDING THE MATCHING FIGURE

DIRECTIONS: Find the figure on this page that matches the figure on the page before. Do not look back at the page before.

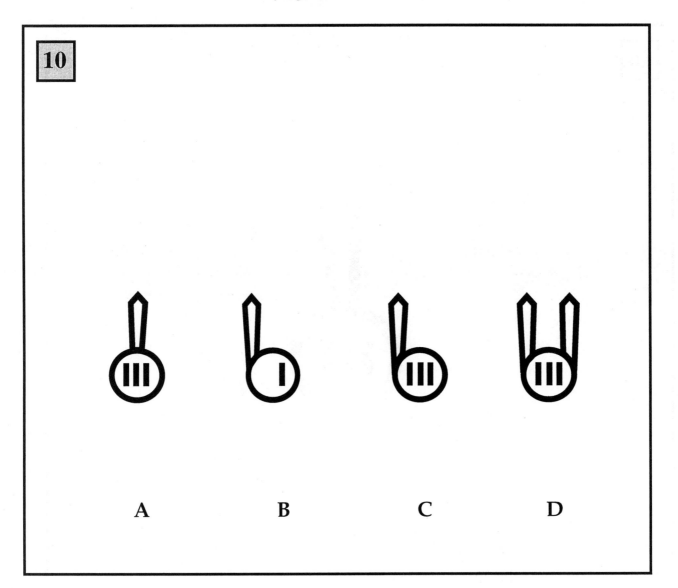

FINDING THE MATCHING FIGURE

DIRECTIONS: Look at the figure on this page. Then turn the page and find the matching figure. Do not look back at this page.

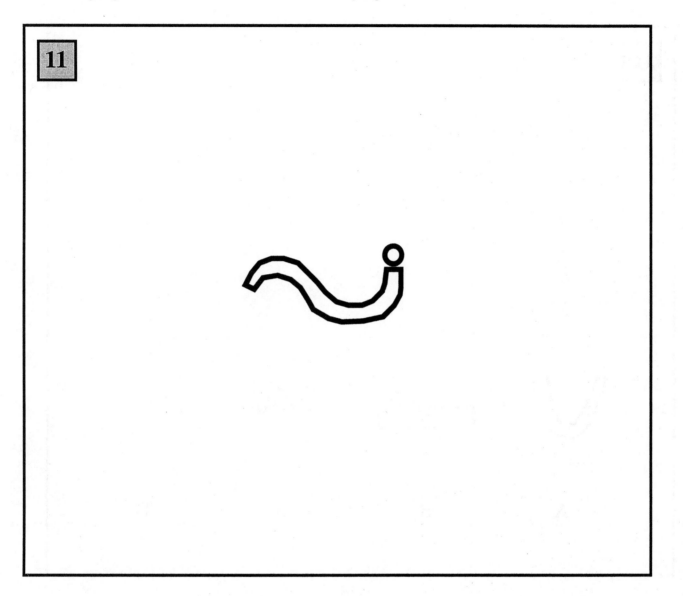

FINDING THE MATCHING FIGURE

DIRECTIONS: Find the figure on this page that matches the figure on the page before. Do not look back at the page before.

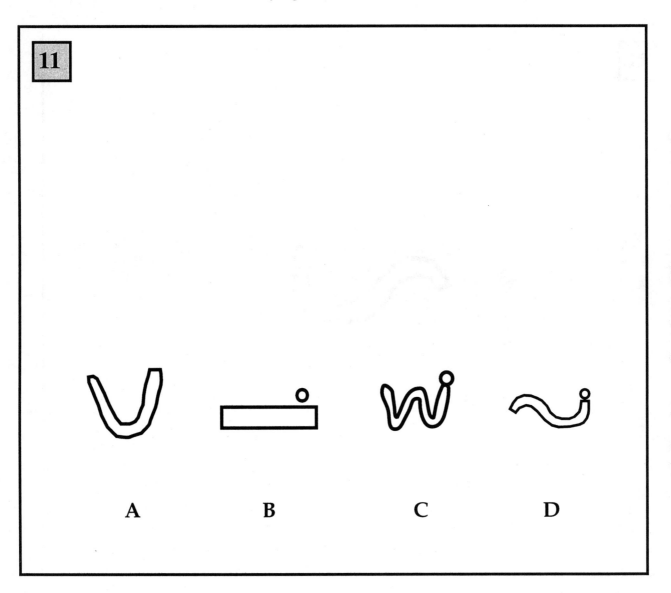

FINDING THE MATCHING FIGURE

DIRECTIONS: Look at the figure on this page. Then turn the page and find the matching figure. Do not look back at this page.

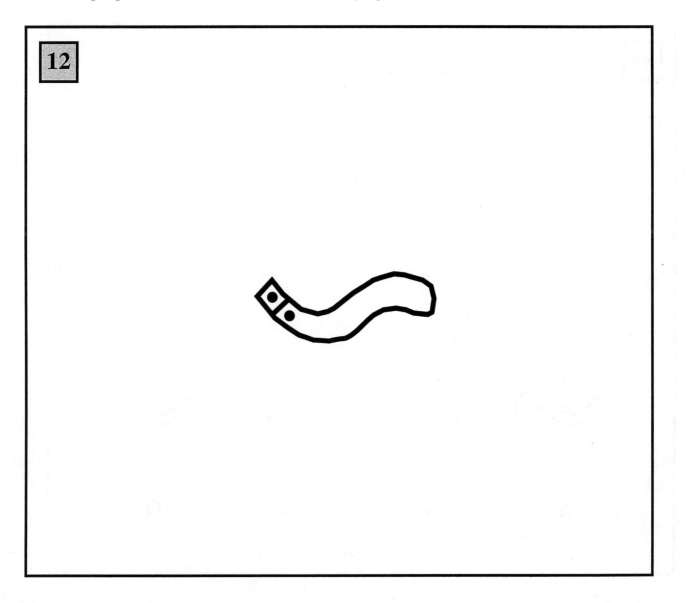

FINDING THE MATCHING FIGURE

DIRECTIONS: Find the figure on this page that matches the figure on the page before. Do not look back at the page before.

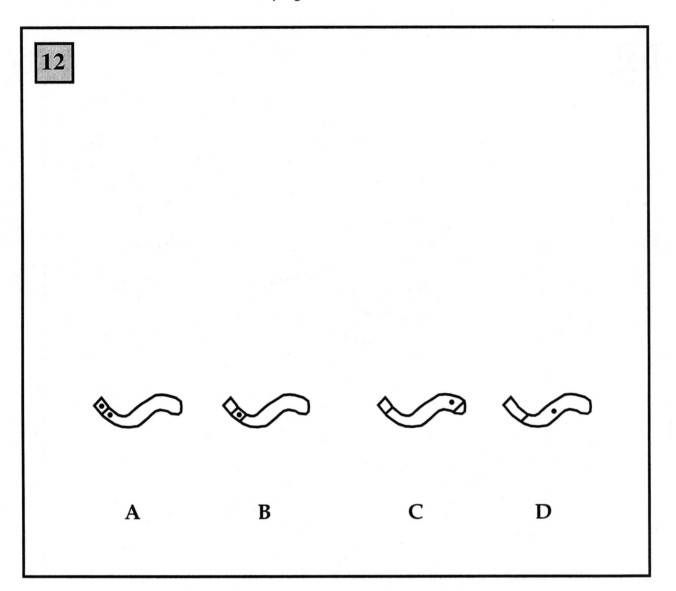

FINDING THE MATCHING FIGURE

DIRECTIONS: Look at the figure on this page. Then turn the page and find the matching figure. Do not look back at this page.

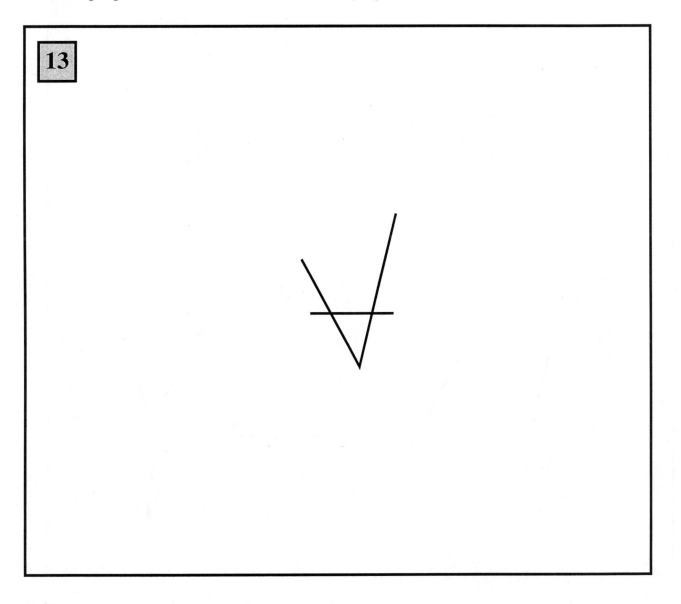

FINDING THE MATCHING FIGURE

DIRECTIONS: Find the figure on this page that matches the figure on the page before. Do not look back at the page before.

FINDING THE MATCHING FIGURE

DIRECTIONS: Look at the figure on this page. Then turn the page and find the matching figure. Do not look back at this page.

FINDING THE MATCHING FIGURE

DIRECTIONS: Find the figure on this page that matches the figure on the page before. Do not look back at the page before.

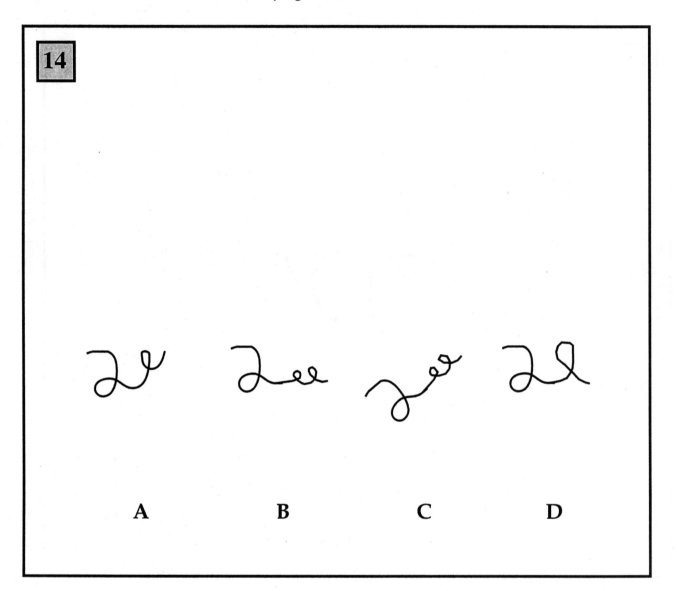

14

A   B   C   D

FINDING THE MATCHING FIGURE

DIRECTIONS: Look at the figure on this page. Then turn the page and find the matching figure. Do not look back at this page.

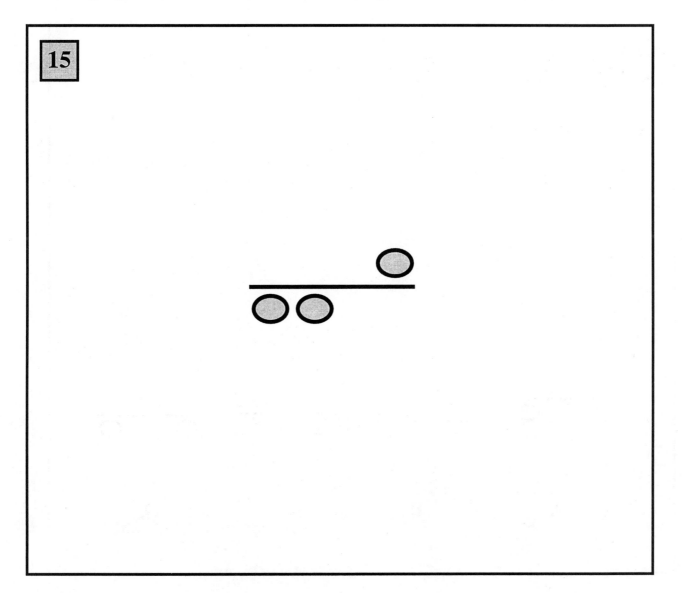

FINDING THE MATCHING FIGURE

DIRECTIONS: Find the figure on this page that matches the figure on the page before. Do not look back at the page before.

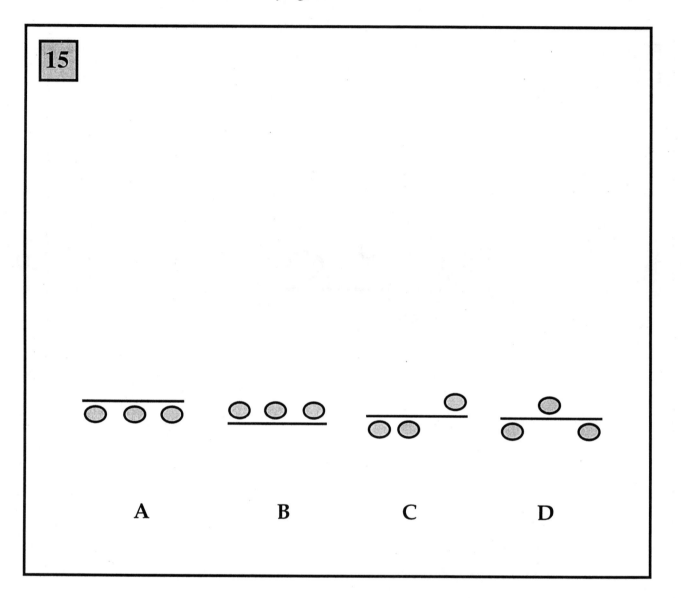

FINDING THE MATCHING FIGURE

DIRECTIONS: Look at the figure on this page. Then turn the page and find the matching figure. Do not look back at this page.

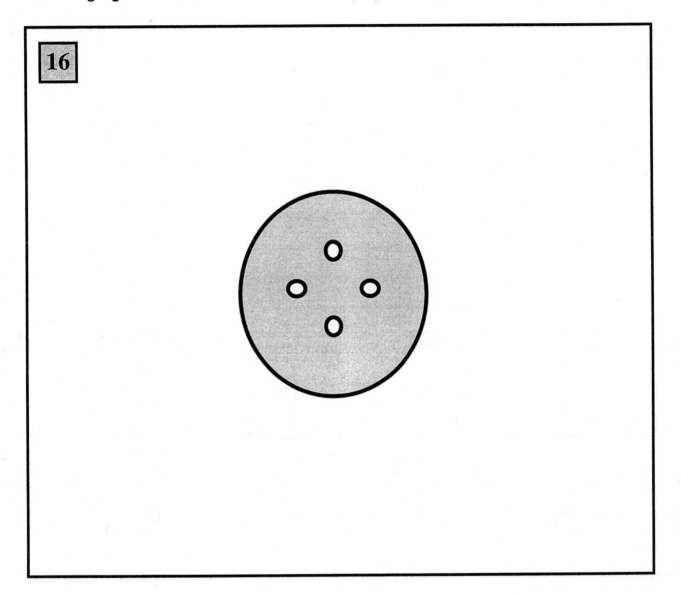

FINDING THE MATCHING FIGURE

DIRECTIONS: Find the figure on this page that matches the figure on the page before. Do not look back at the page before.

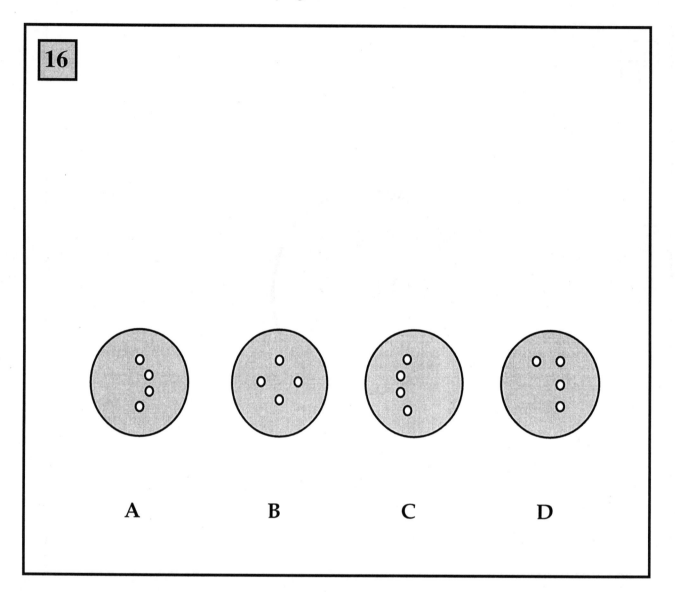

FINDING THE MATCHING FIGURE

DIRECTIONS: Look at the figure on this page. Then turn the page and find the matching figure. Do not look back at this page.

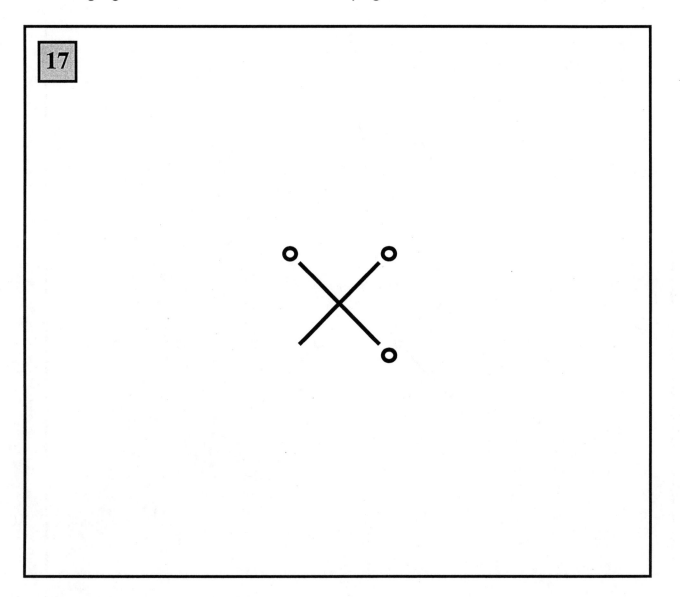

FINDING THE MATCHING FIGURE

DIRECTIONS: Find the figure on this page that matches the figure on the page before. Do not look back at the page before.

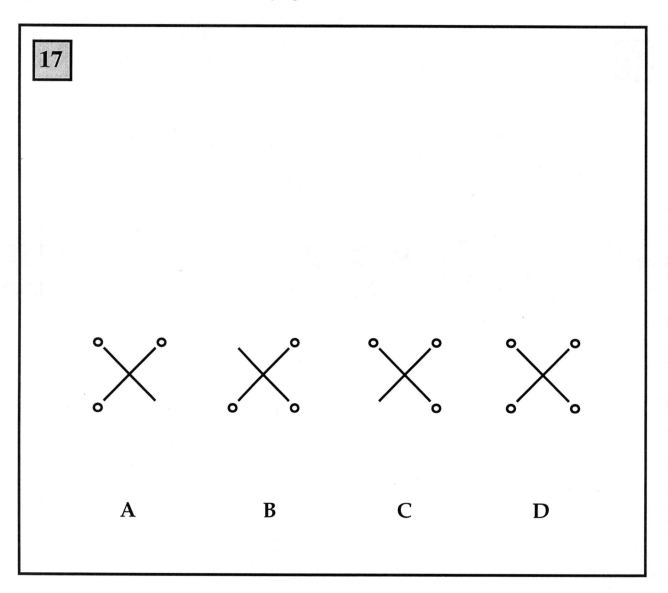

FINDING THE MATCHING FIGURE

DIRECTIONS: Look at the figure on this page. Then turn the page and find the matching figure. Do not look back at this page.

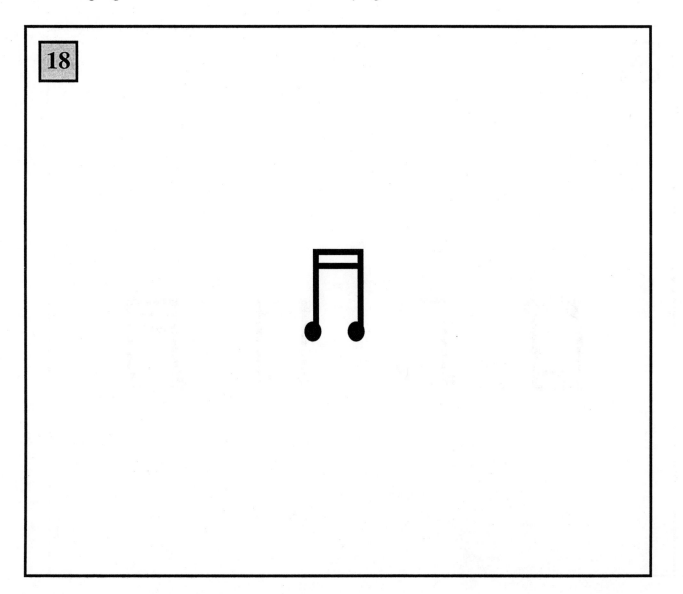

FINDING THE MATCHING FIGURE

DIRECTIONS: Find the figure on this page that matches the figure on the page before. Do not look back at the page before.

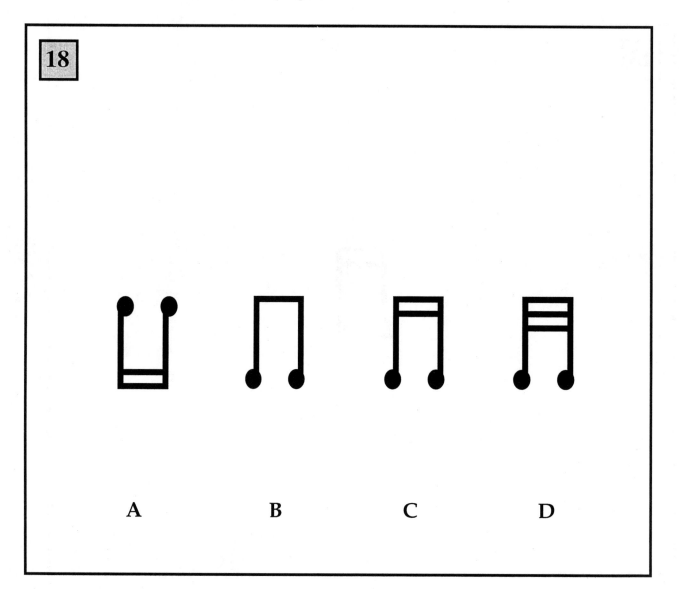

FINDING THE MATCHING FIGURE

DIRECTIONS: Look at the figure on this page. Then turn the page and find the matching figure. Do not look back at this page.

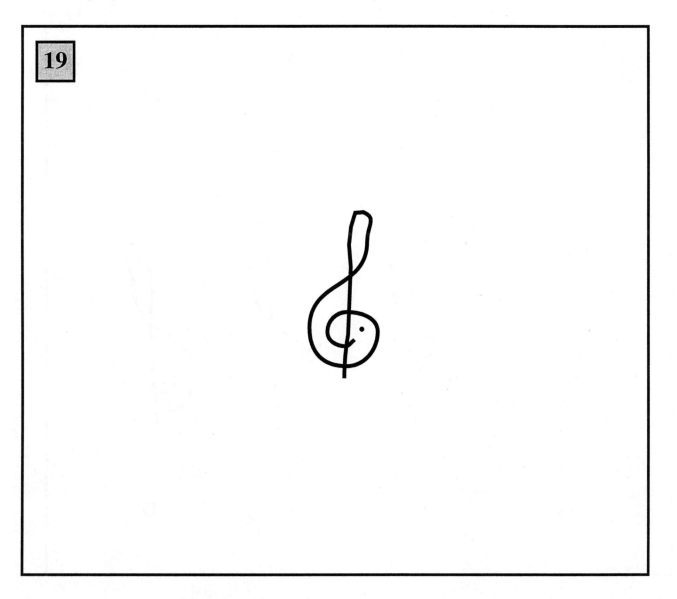

FINDING THE MATCHING FIGURE

DIRECTIONS: Find the figure on this page that matches the figure on the page before. Do not look back at the page before.

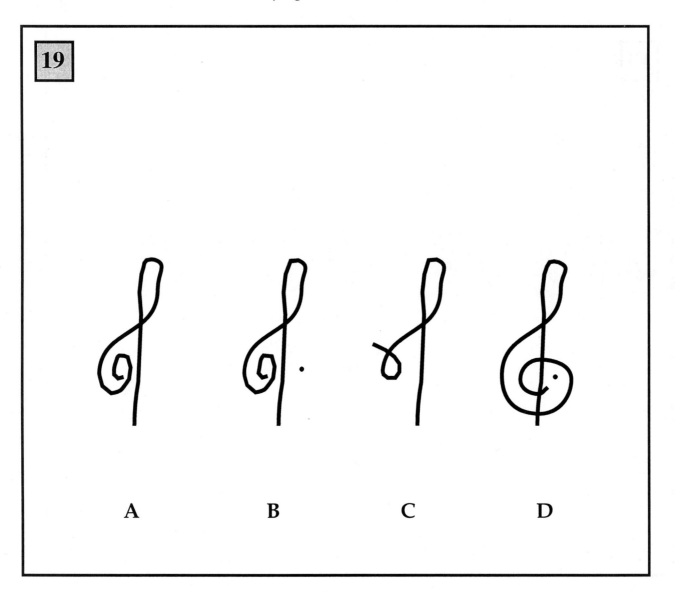

19

A   B   C   D

FINDING THE MATCHING FIGURE

DIRECTIONS: Look at the figure on this page. Then turn the page and find the matching figure. Do not look back at this page.

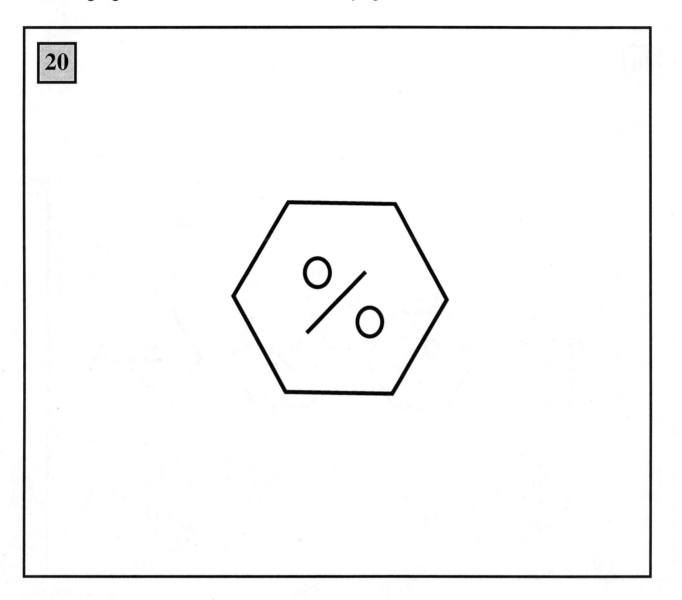

FINDING THE MATCHING FIGURE

DIRECTIONS: Find the figure on this page that matches the figure on the page before. Do not look back at the page before.

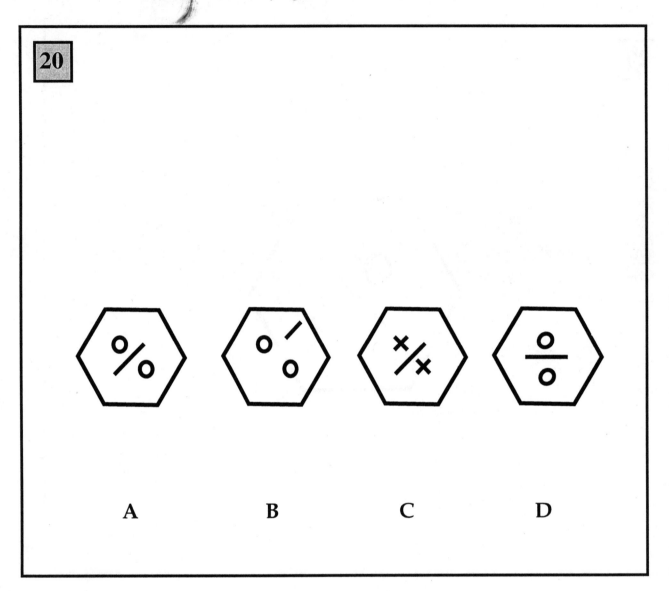

VISUAL SEQUENTIAL MEMORY PRETEST

DIRECTIONS: Look at the order of the figures on this page. Then find the set of figures with the same order on the next page. Do not look back at this page.

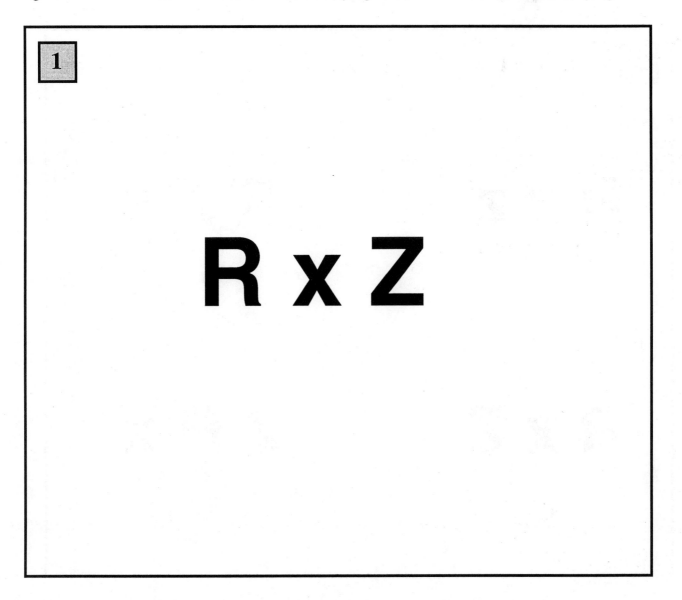

VISUAL SEQUENTIAL MEMORY PRETEST

DIRECTIONS: Find the figures on this page that are in the same order as the figures on the page before. Do not look back at the page before.

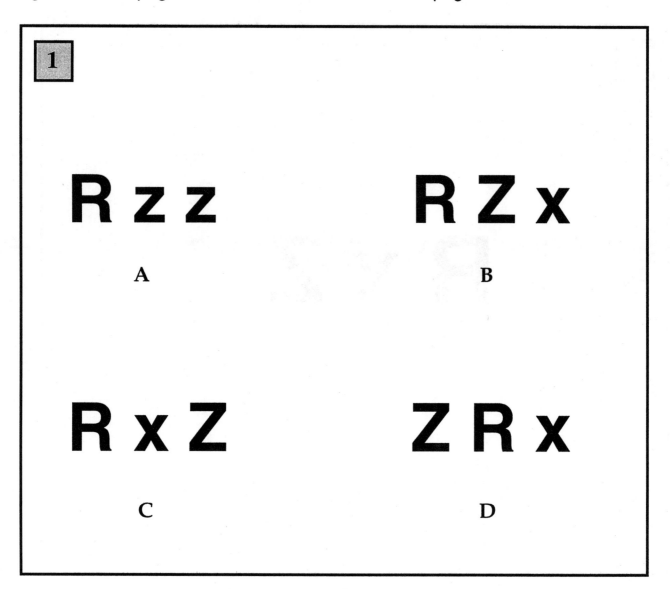

VISUAL SEQUENTIAL MEMORY PRETEST

DIRECTIONS: Look at the order of the figures on this page. Then find the set of figures with the same order on the next page. Do not look back at this page.

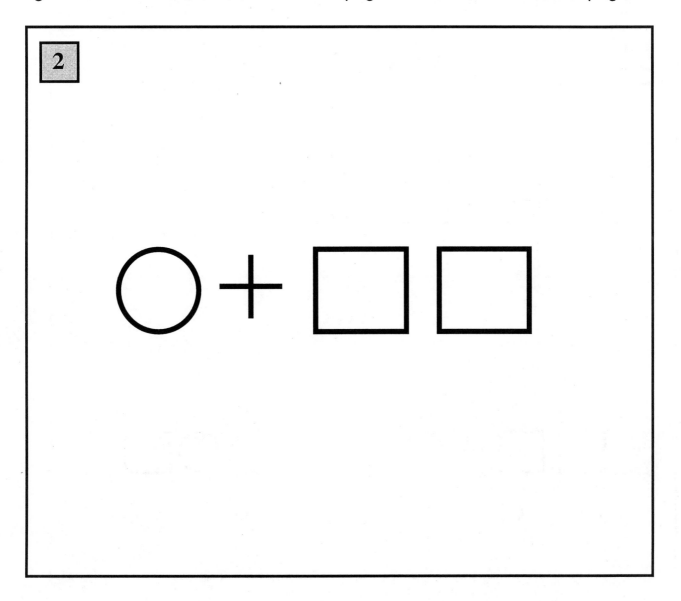

VISUAL SEQUENTIAL MEMORY PRETEST

DIRECTIONS: Find the figures on this page that are in the same order as the figures on the page before. Do not look back at the page before.

2

○ + ▢ ▢

A

▢ ○ + ▢

B

▢ ▢ + ○

C

+ ▢ ○ ▢

D

VISUAL SEQUENTIAL MEMORY PRETEST

DIRECTIONS: Look at the order of the figures on this page. Then find the set of figures with the same order on the next page. Do not look back at this page.

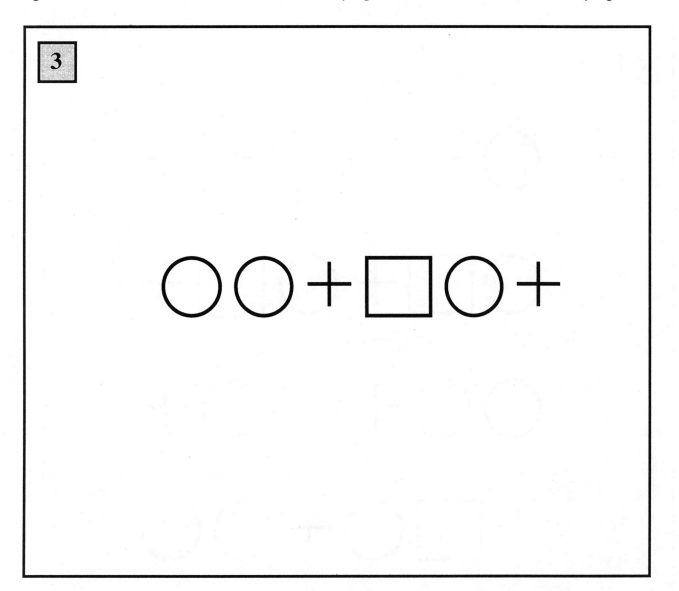

VISUAL SEQUENTIAL MEMORY PRETEST

DIRECTIONS: Find the figures on this page that are in the same order as the figures on the page before. Do not look back at the page before.

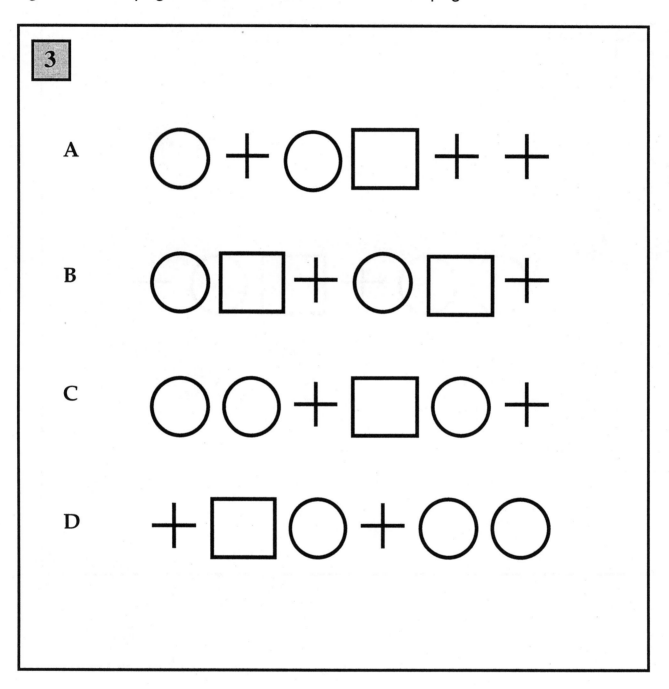

VISUAL SEQUENTIAL MEMORY POSTTEST

DIRECTIONS: Look at the order of the figures on this page. Then find the set of figures with the same order on the next page. Do not look back at this page.

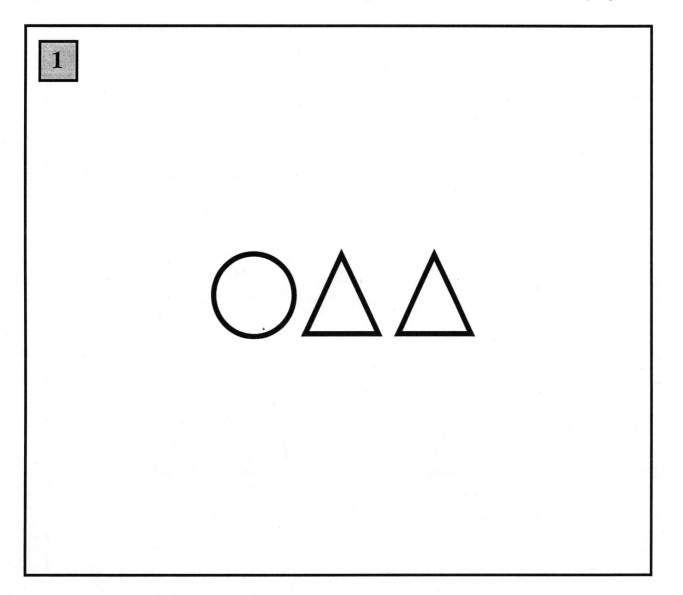

VISUAL SEQUENTIAL MEMORY POSTTEST

DIRECTIONS: Find the figures on this page that are in the same order as the figures on the page before. Do not look back at the page before.

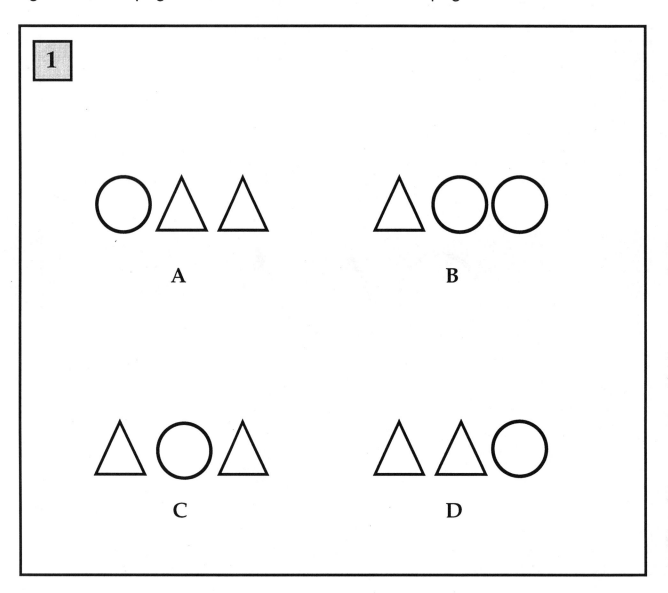

VISUAL SEQUENTIAL MEMORY POSTTEST

DIRECTIONS: Look at the order of the figures on this page. Then find the set of figures with the same order on the next page. Do not look back at this page.

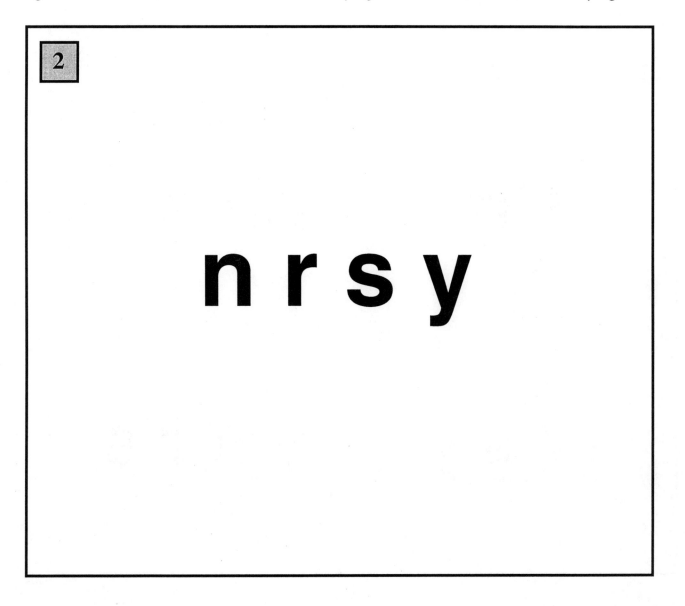

VISUAL SEQUENTIAL MEMORY POSTTEST

DIRECTIONS: Find the figures on this page that are in the same order as the figures on the page before. Do not look back at the page before.

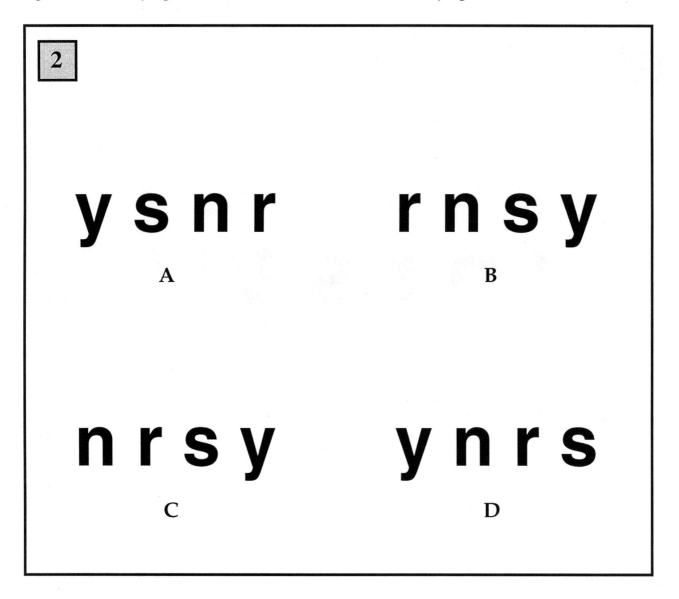

VISUAL SEQUENTIAL MEMORY POSTTEST

DIRECTIONS: Look at the order of the figures on this page. Then find the set of figures with the same order on the next page. Do not look back at this page.

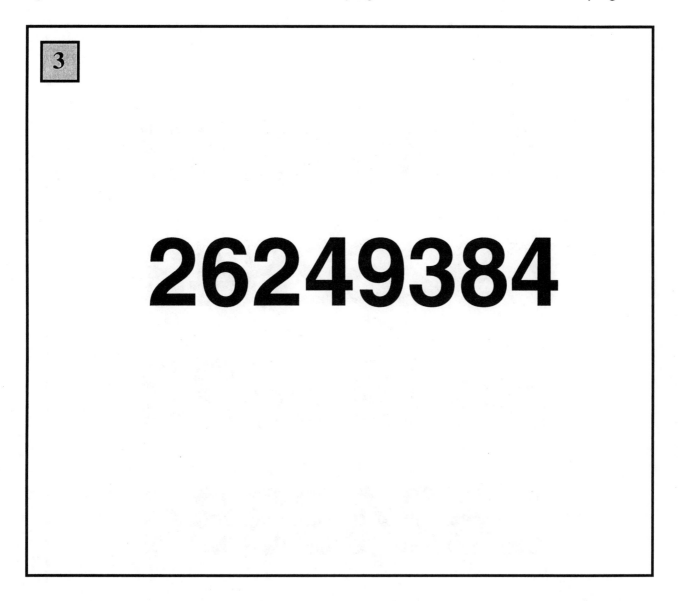

VISUAL SEQUENTIAL MEMORY POSTTEST

DIRECTIONS: Find the figures on this page that are in the same order as the figures on the page before. Do not look back at the page before.

3

A **48394262**

B **49262843**

C **84492623**

D **26249384**

FINDING THE MATCHING FIGURES

DIRECTIONS: Look at the order of the figures on this page. Then find the set of figures with the same order on the next page. Do not look back at this page.

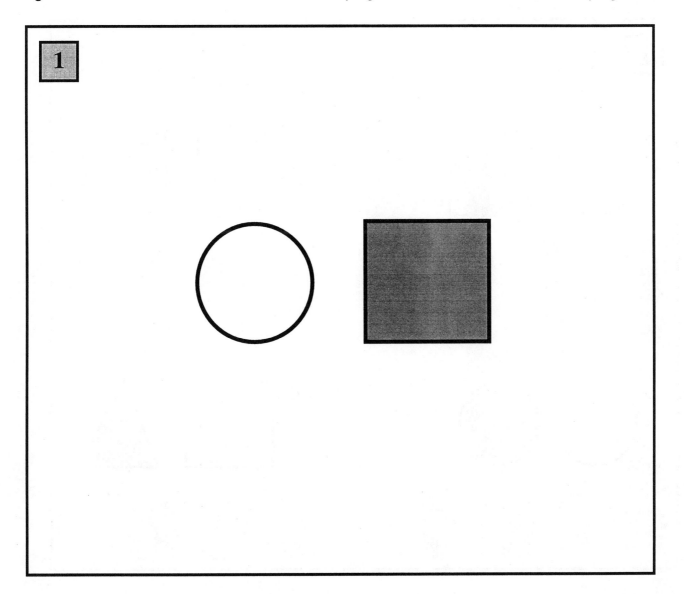

FINDING THE MATCHING FIGURES

DIRECTIONS: Find the figures on this page that are in the same order as the figures on the page before. Do not look back at the page before.

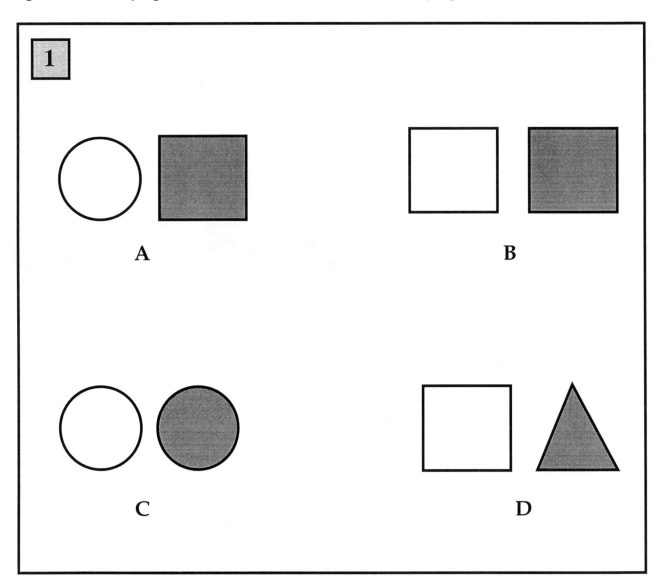

FINDING THE MATCHING FIGURES

DIRECTIONS: Look at the order of the figures on this page. Then find the set of figures with the same order on the next page. Do not look back at this page.

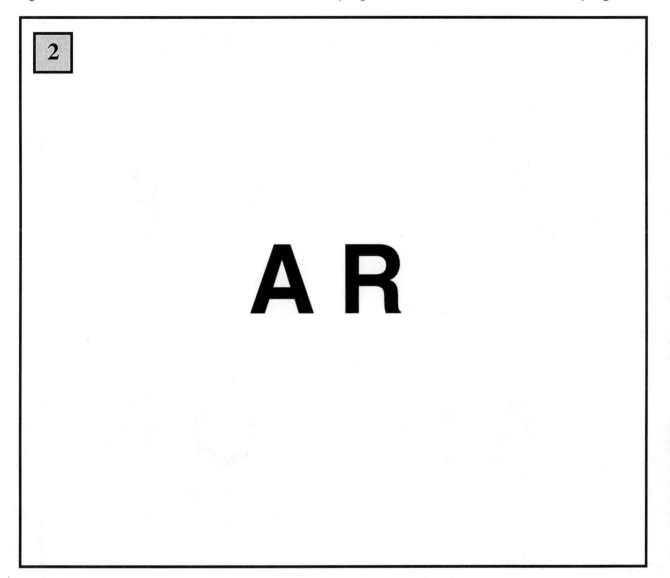

FINDING THE MATCHING FIGURES

DIRECTIONS: Find the figures on this page that are in the same order as the figures on the page before. Do not look back at the page before.

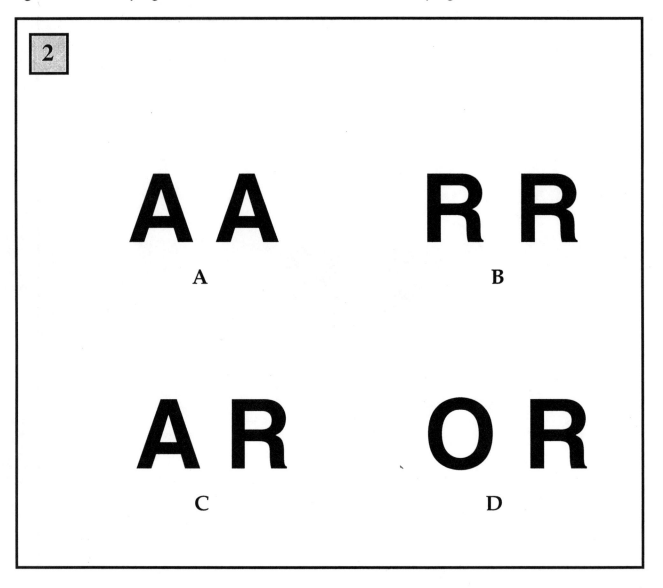

FINDING THE MATCHING FIGURES

DIRECTIONS: Look at the order of the figures on this page. Then find the set of figures with the same order on the next page. Do not look back at this page.

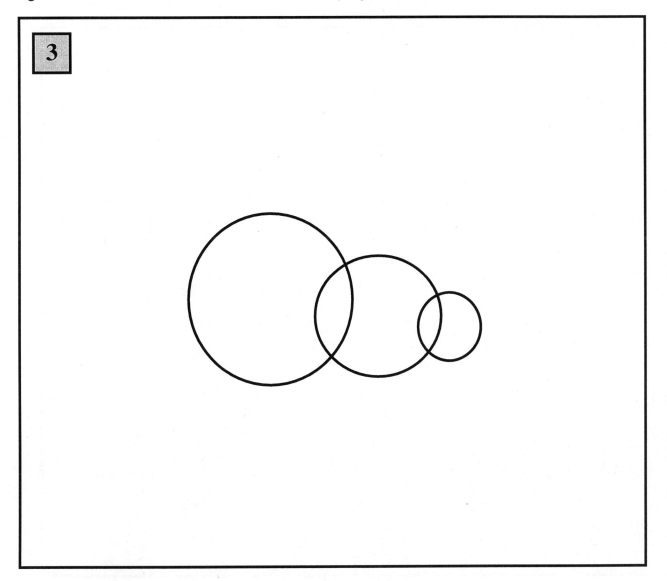

FINDING THE MATCHING FIGURES

DIRECTIONS: Find the figures on this page that are in the same order as the figures on the page before. Do not look back at the page before.

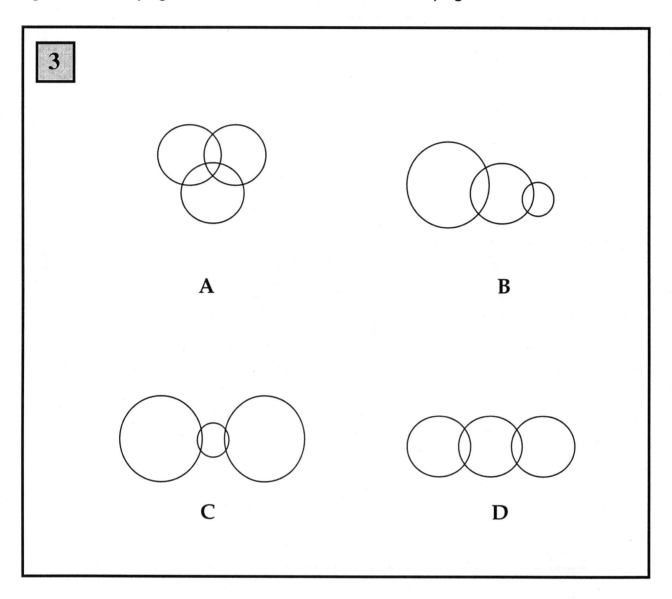

FINDING THE MATCHING FIGURES

DIRECTIONS: Look at the order of the figures on this page. Then find the set of figures with the same order on the next page. Do not look back at this page.

FINDING THE MATCHING FIGURES

DIRECTIONS: Find the figures on this page that are in the same order as the figures on the page before. Do not look back at the page before.

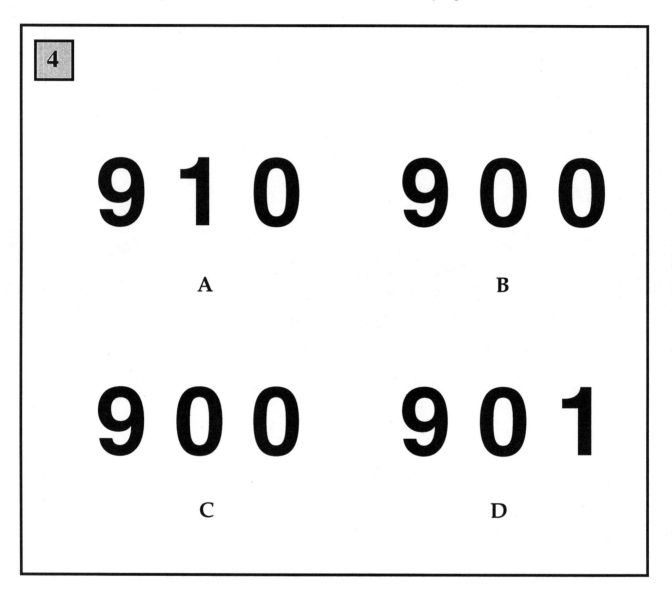

4

910   900

A   B

900   901

C   D

FINDING THE MATCHING FIGURES

DIRECTIONS: Look at the order of the figures on this page. Then find the set of figures with the same order on the next page. Do not look back at this page.

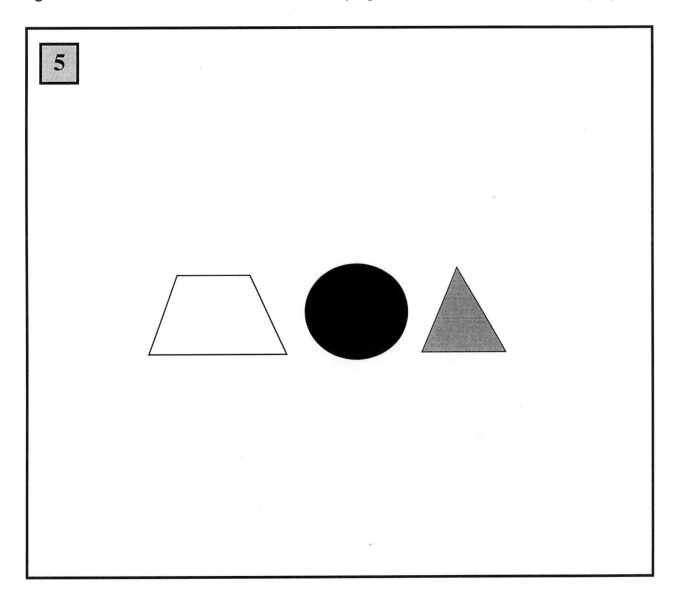

FINDING THE MATCHING FIGURES

DIRECTIONS: Find the figures on this page that are in the same order as the figures on the page before. Do not look back at the page before.

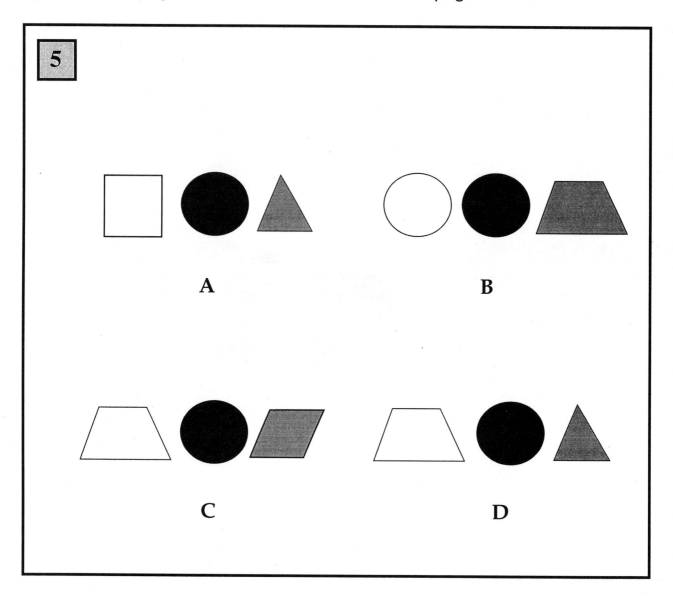

FINDING THE MATCHING FIGURES

DIRECTIONS: Look at the order of the figures on this page. Then find the set of figures with the same order on the next page. Do not look back at this page.

FINDING THE MATCHING FIGURES

DIRECTIONS: Find the figures on this page that are in the same order as the figures on the page before. Do not look back at the page before.

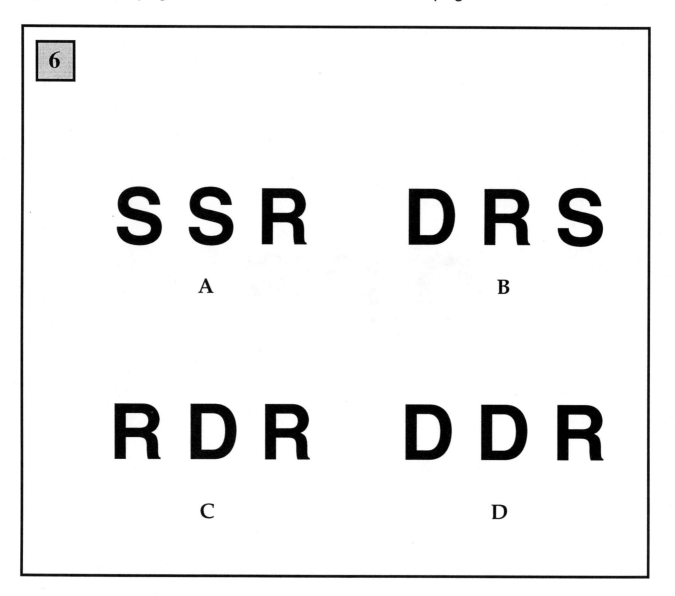

FINDING THE MATCHING FIGURES

DIRECTIONS: Look at the order of the figures on this page. Then find the set of figures with the same order on the next page. Do not look back at this page.

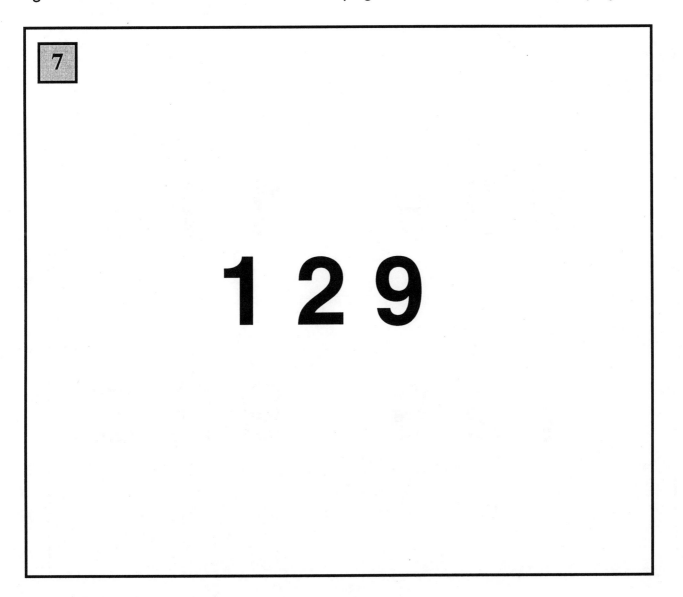

7

1 2 9

FINDING THE MATCHING FIGURES

DIRECTIONS: Find the figures on this page that are in the same order as the figures on the page before. Do not look back at the page before.

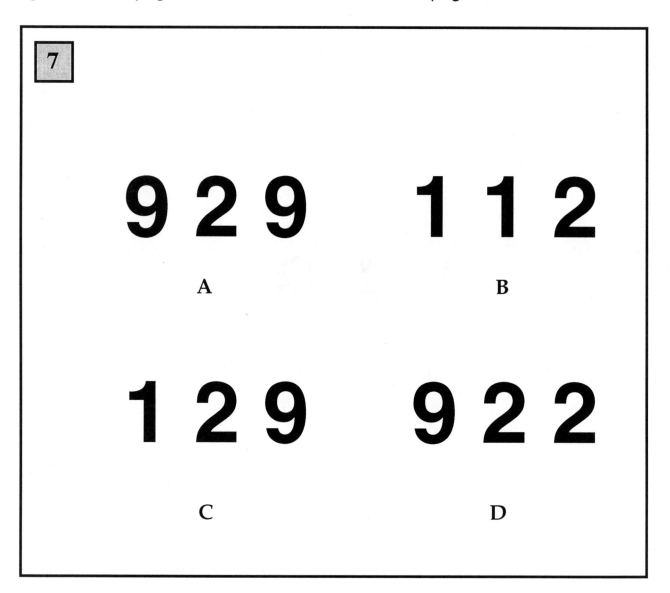

FINDING THE MATCHING FIGURES

DIRECTIONS: Look at the order of the figures on this page. Then find the set of figures with the same order on the next page. Do not look back at this page.

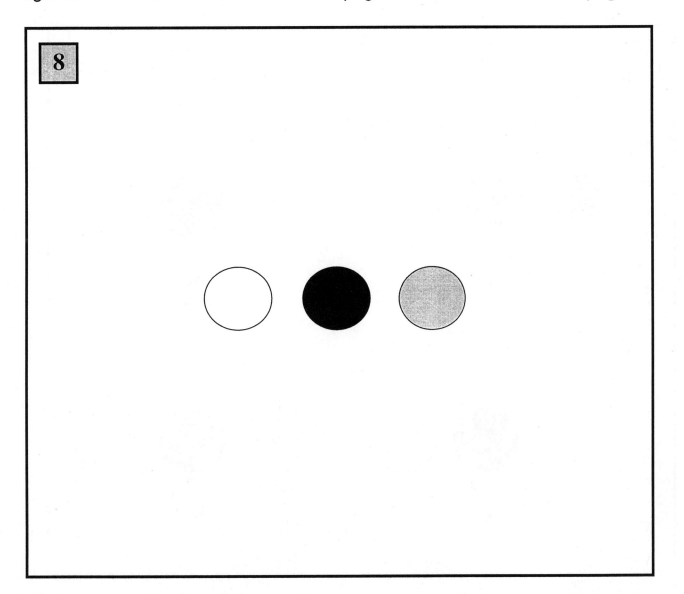

FINDING THE MATCHING FIGURES

DIRECTIONS: Find the figures on this page that are in the same order as the figures on the page before. Do not look back at the page before.

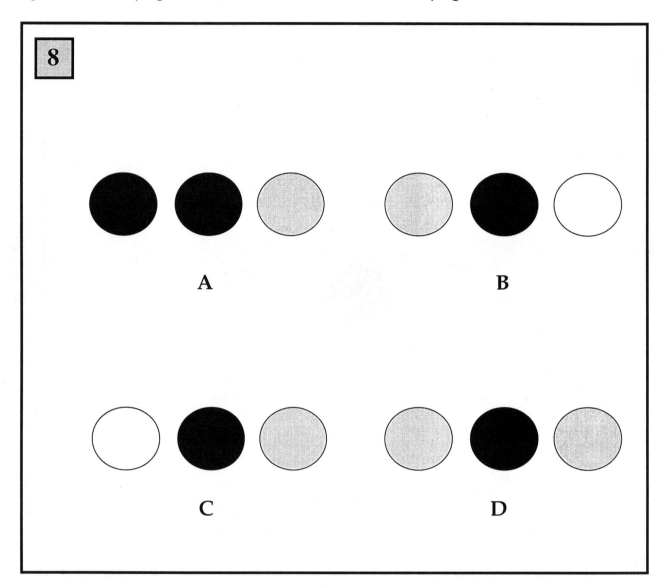

FINDING THE MATCHING FIGURES

DIRECTIONS: Look at the order of the figures on this page. Then find the set of figures with the same order on the next page. Do not look back at this page.

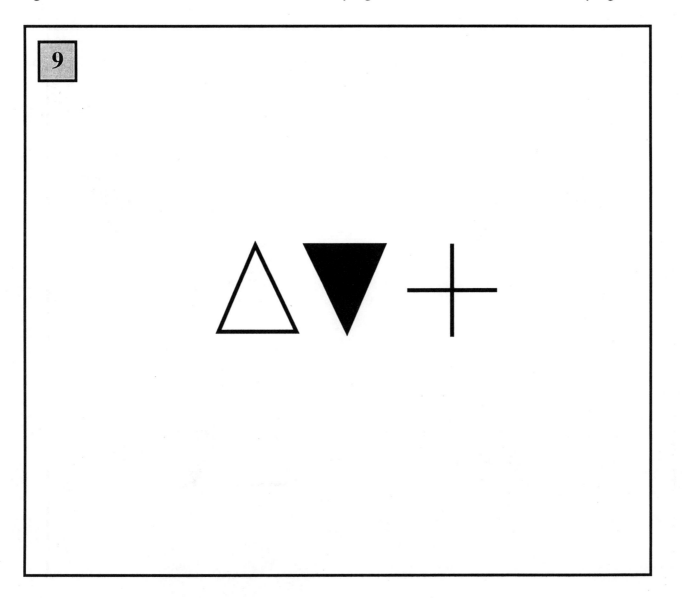

FINDING THE MATCHING FIGURES

DIRECTIONS: Find the figures on this page that are in the same order as the figures on the page before. Do not look back at the page before.

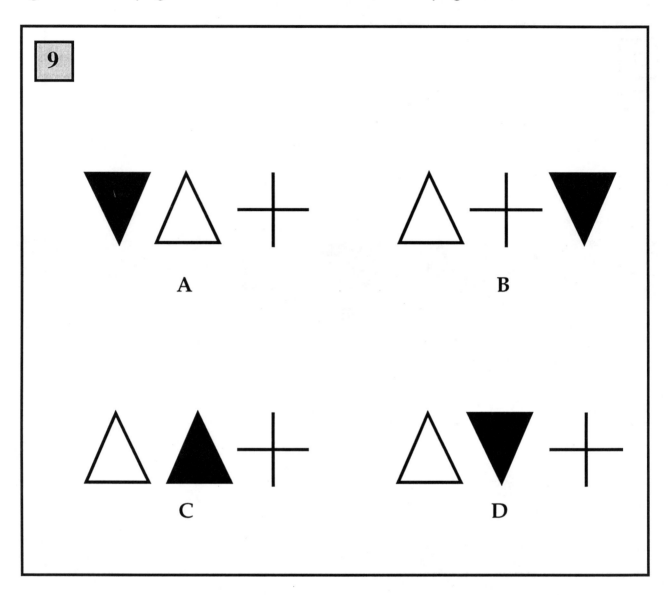

FINDING THE MATCHING FIGURES

DIRECTIONS: Look at the order of the figures on this page. Then find the set of figures with the same order on the next page. Do not look back at this page.

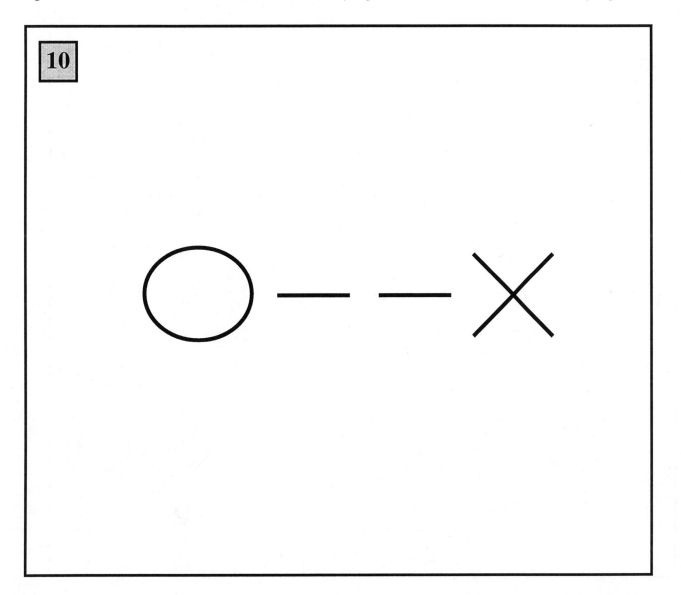

FINDING THE MATCHING FIGURES

DIRECTIONS: Find the figures on this page that are in the same order as the figures on the page before. Do not look back at the page before.

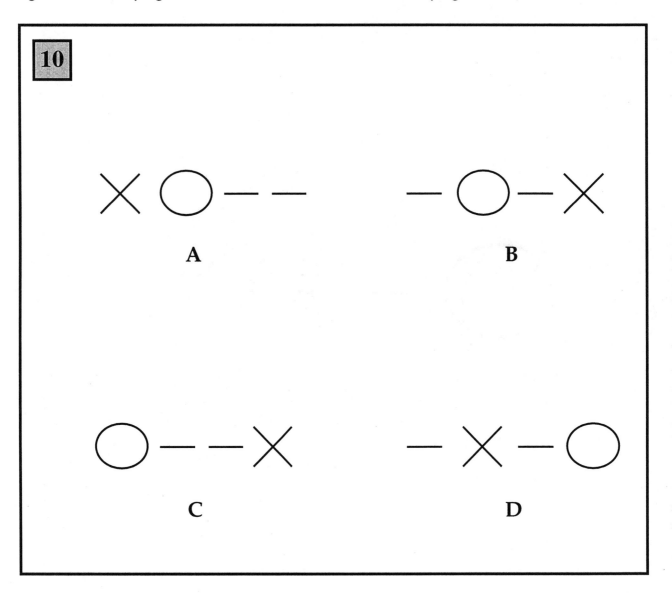

FINDING THE MATCHING FIGURES

DIRECTIONS: Look at the order of the figures on this page. Then find the set of figures with the same order on the next page. Do not look back at this page.

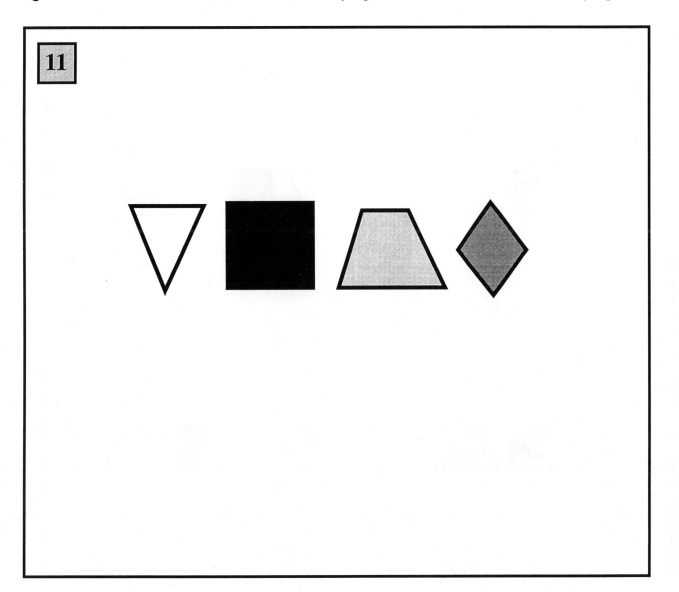

FINDING THE MATCHING FIGURES

DIRECTIONS: Find the figures on this page that are in the same order as the figures on the page before. Do not look back at the page before.

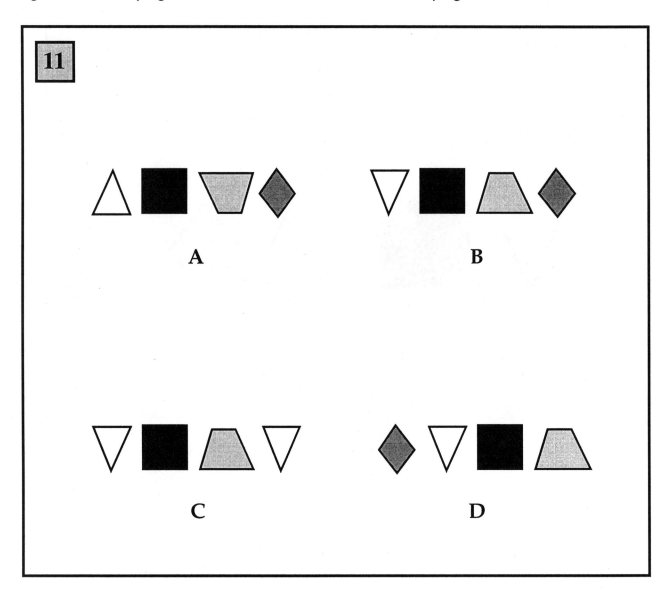

FINDING THE MATCHING FIGURES

DIRECTIONS: Look at the order of the figures on this page. Then find the set of figures with the same order on the next page. Do not look back at this page.

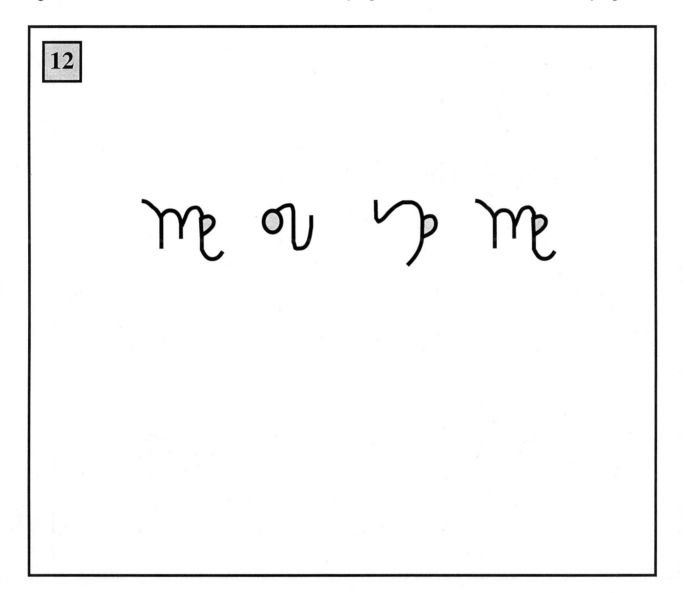

FINDING THE MATCHING FIGURES

DIRECTIONS: Find the figures on this page that are in the same order as the figures on the page before. Do not look back at the page before.

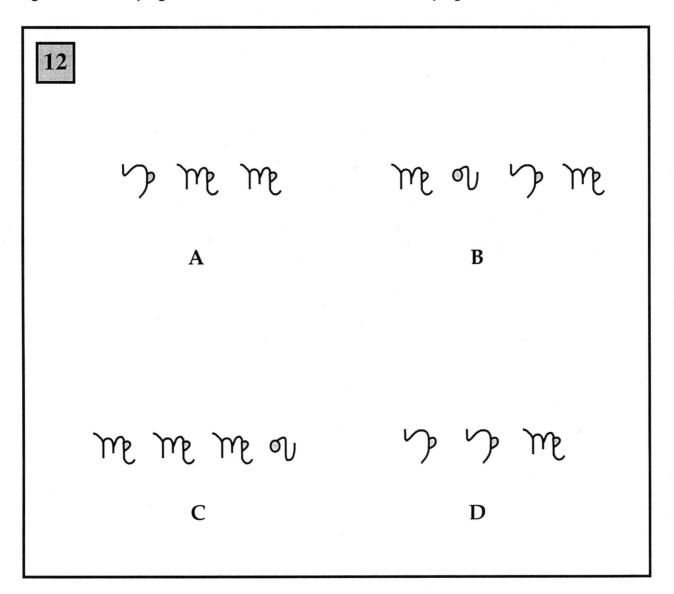

© 1998 CRITICAL THINKING BOOKS & SOFTWARE • WWW.CRITICALTHINKING.COM • 800-458-4849

FINDING THE MATCHING FIGURES

DIRECTIONS: Look at the order of the figures on this page. Then find the set of figures with the same order on the next page. Do not look back at this page.

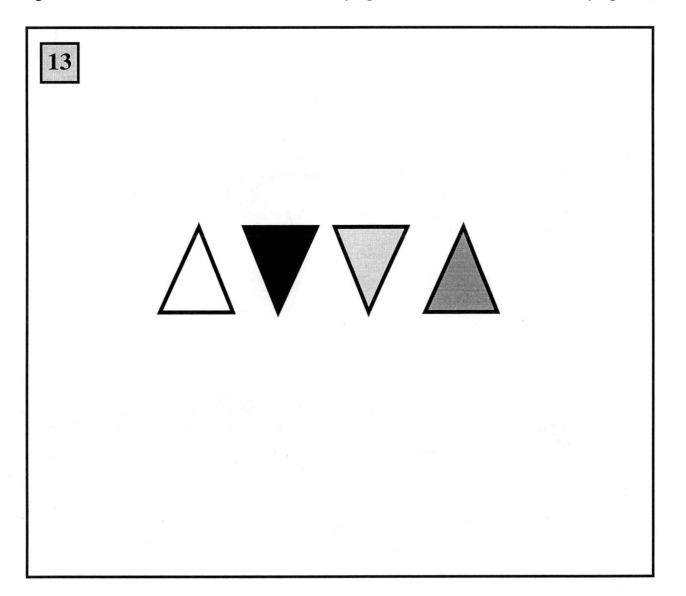

FINDING THE MATCHING FIGURES

DIRECTIONS: Find the figures on this page that are in the same order as the figures on the page before. Do not look back at the page before.

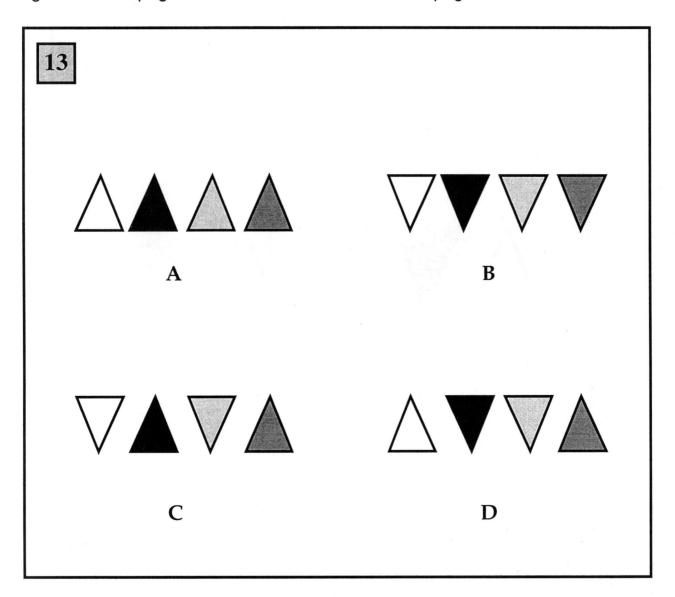

FINDING THE MATCHING FIGURES

DIRECTIONS: Look at the order of the figures on this page. Then find the set of figures with the same order on the next page. Do not look back at this page.

FINDING THE MATCHING FIGURES

DIRECTIONS: Find the figures on this page that are in the same order as the figures on the page before. Do not look back at the page before.

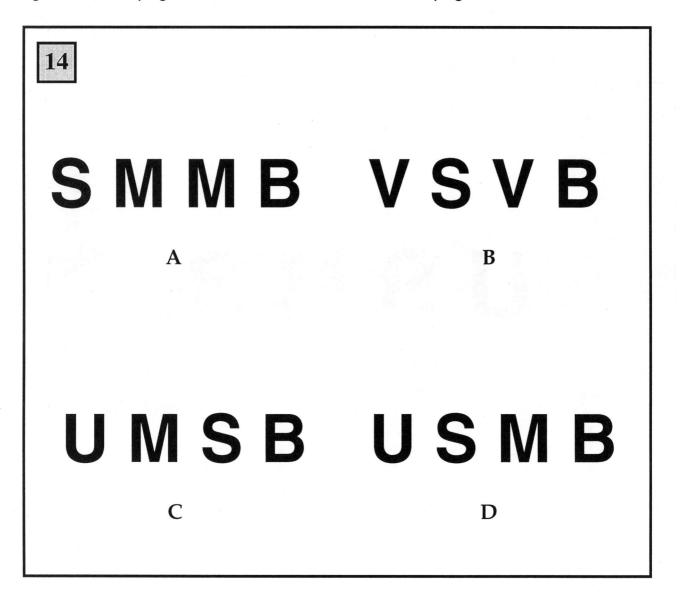

© 1998 CRITICAL THINKING BOOKS & SOFTWARE • WWW.CRITICALTHINKING.COM • 800-458-4849

FINDING THE MATCHING FIGURES

DIRECTIONS: Look at the order of the figures on this page. Then find the set of figures with the same order on the next page. Do not look back at this page.

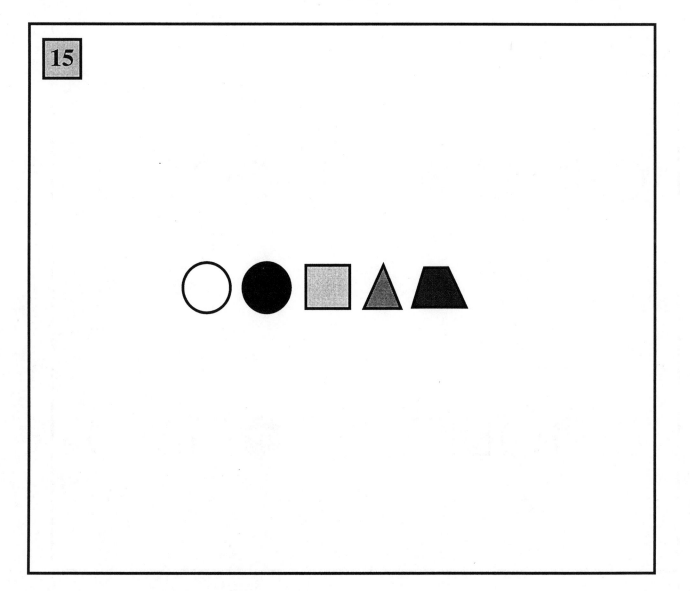

FINDING THE MATCHING FIGURES

DIRECTIONS: Find the figures on this page that are in the same order as the figures on the page before. Do not look back at the page before.

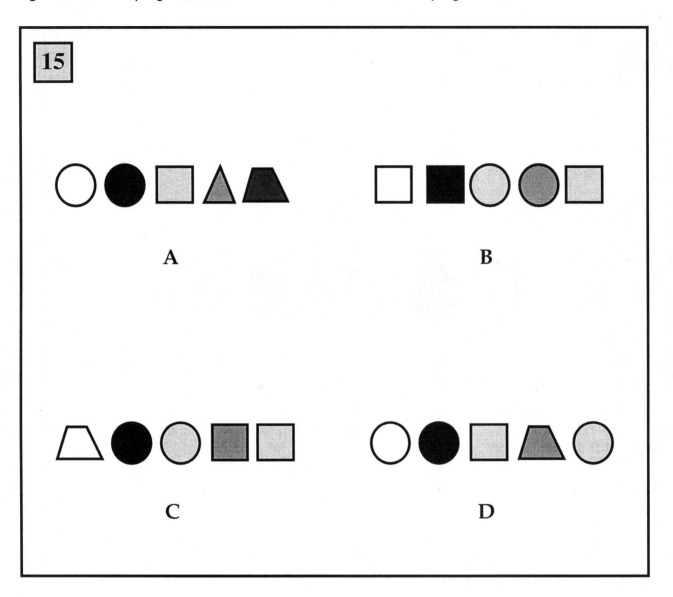

FINDING THE MATCHING FIGURES

DIRECTIONS: Look at the order of the figures on this page. Then find the set of figures with the same order on the next page. Do not look back at this page.

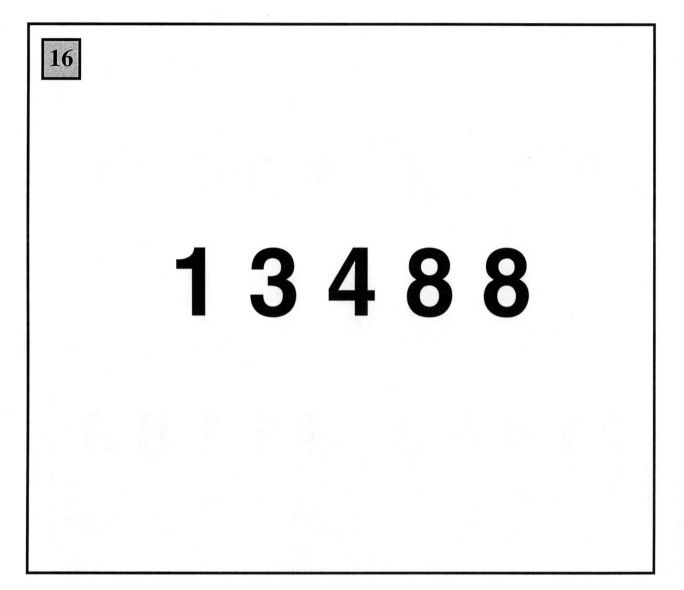

16

1 3 4 8 8

FINDING THE MATCHING FIGURES

DIRECTIONS: Find the figures on this page that are in the same order as the figures on the page before. Do not look back at the page before.

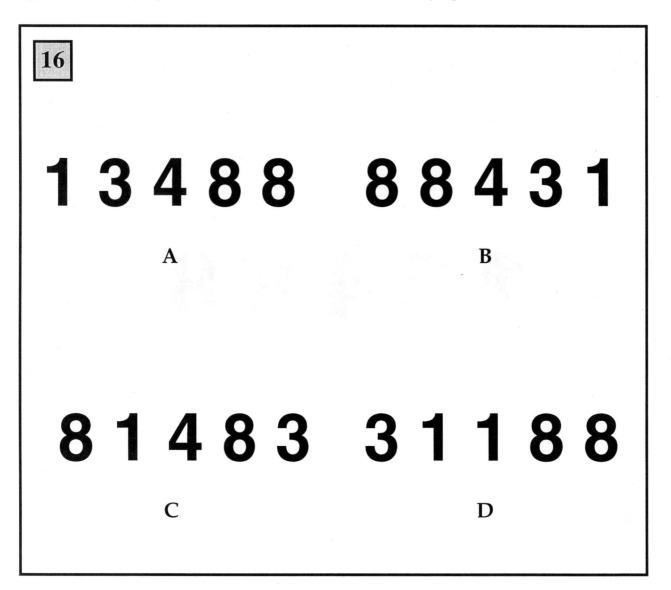

FINDING THE MATCHING FIGURES

DIRECTIONS: Look at the order of the figures on this page. Then find the set of figures with the same order on the next page. Do not look back at this page.

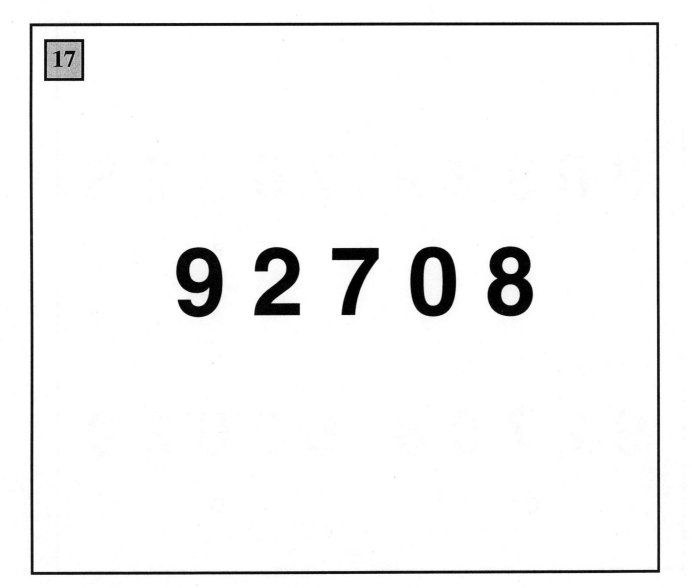

17

9 2 7 0 8

FINDING THE MATCHING FIGURES

DIRECTIONS: Find the figures on this page that are in the same order as the figures on the page before. Do not look back at the page before.

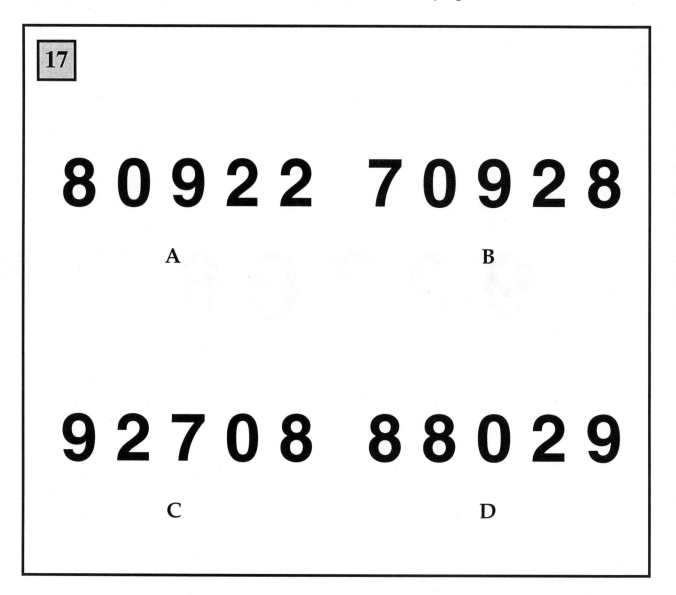

17

8 0 9 2 2   7 0 9 2 8

A   B

9 2 7 0 8   8 8 0 2 9

C   D

FINDING THE MATCHING FIGURES

DIRECTIONS: Look at the order of the figures on this page. Then find the set of figures with the same order on the next page. Do not look back at this page.

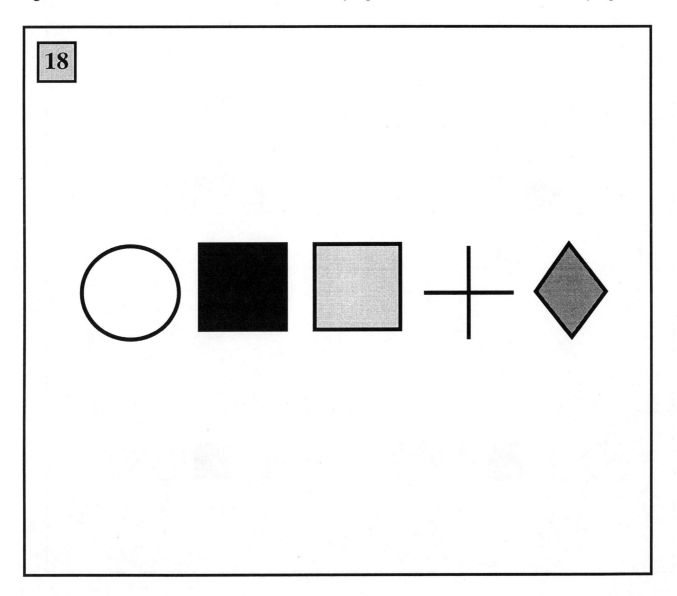

FINDING THE MATCHING FIGURES

DIRECTIONS: Find the figures on this page that are in the same order as the figures on the page before. Do not look back at the page before.

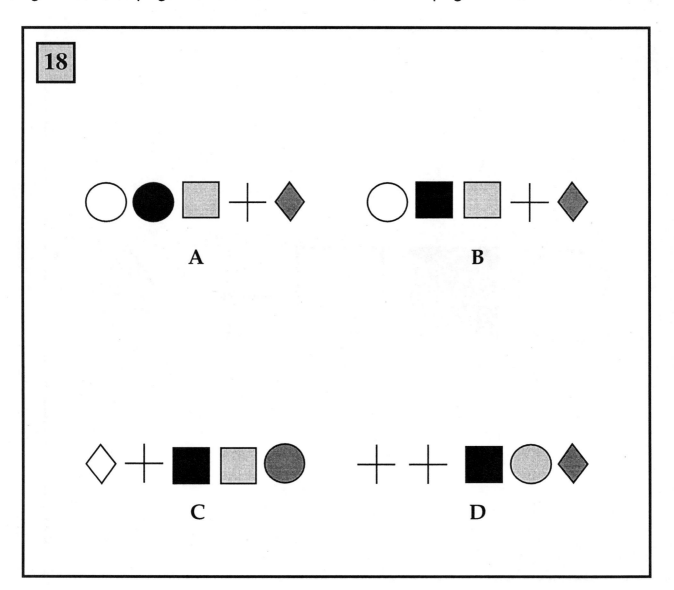

FINDING THE MATCHING FIGURES

DIRECTIONS: Look at the order of the figures on this page. Then find the set of figures with the same order on the next page. Do not look back at this page.

FINDING THE MATCHING FIGURES

DIRECTIONS: Find the figures on this page that are in the same order as the figures on the page before. Do not look back at the page before.

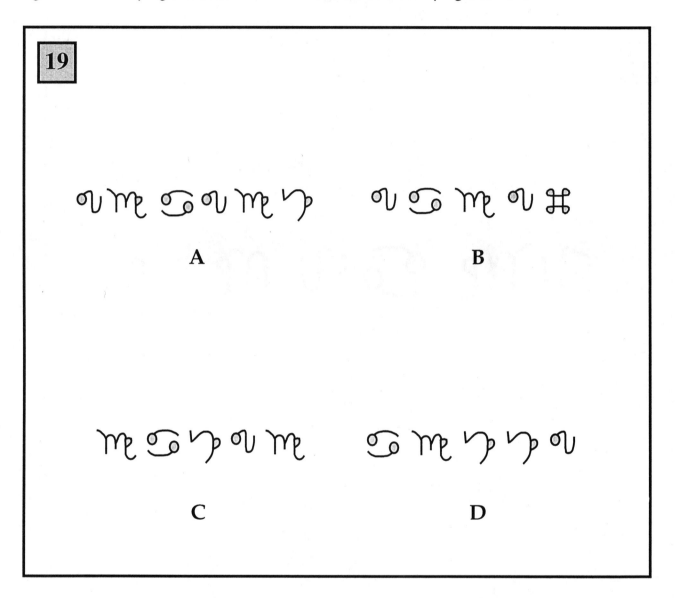

FINDING THE MATCHING FIGURES

DIRECTIONS: Look at the order of the figures on this page. Then find the set of figures with the same order on the next page. Do not look back at this page.

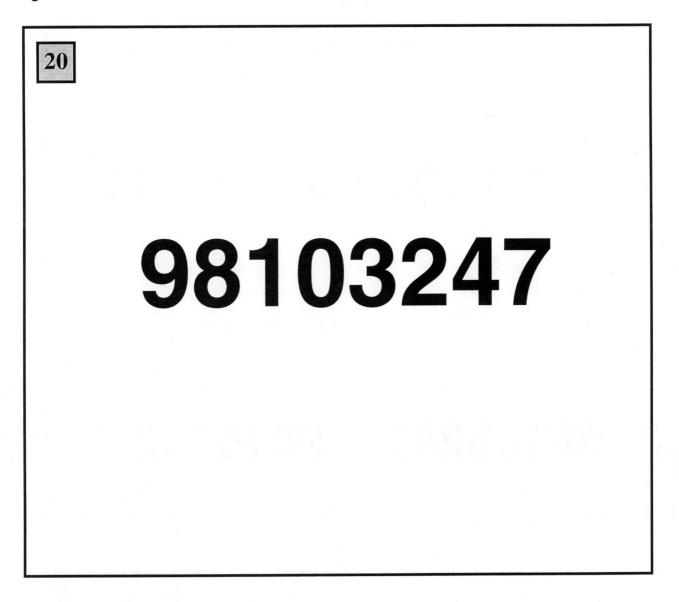

20

98103247

FINDING THE MATCHING FIGURES

DIRECTIONS: Find the figures on this page that are in the same order as the figures on the page before. Do not look back at the page before.

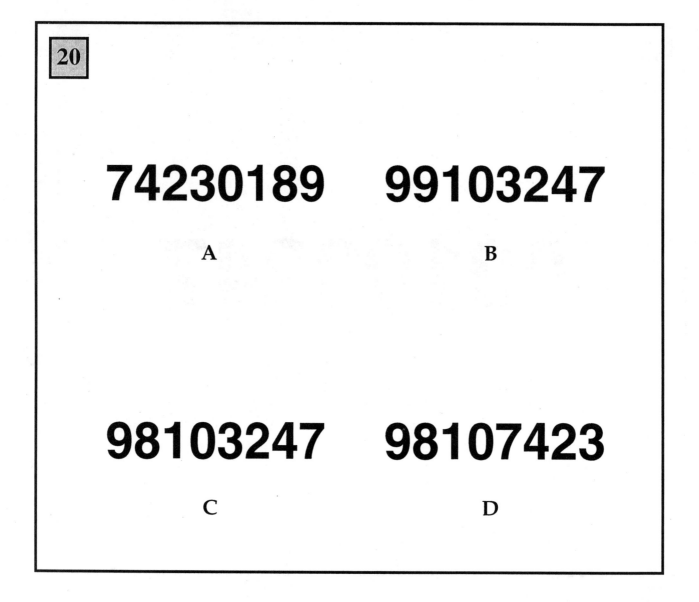

20

74230189   99103247

A   B

98103247   98107423

C   D

FINDING THE MATCHING FIGURES

DIRECTIONS: Find the figures on this page that are in the same order as the figures on the page before. Do not look back at the page before.

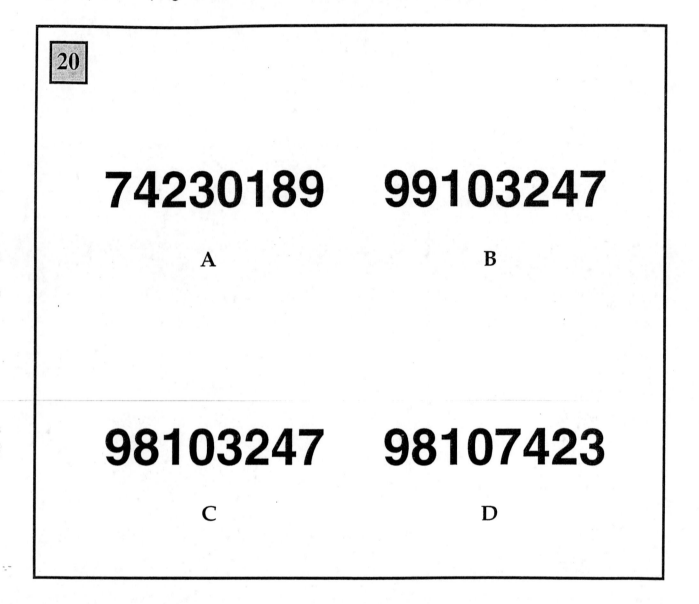

20

74230189   99103247

A   B

98103247   98107423

C   D

VISUAL SPATIAL RELATIONSHIP PRETEST

DIRECTIONS: Find the form that is different and circle it.

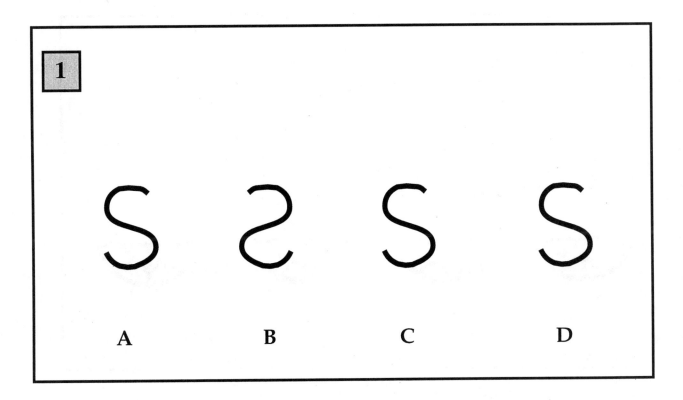

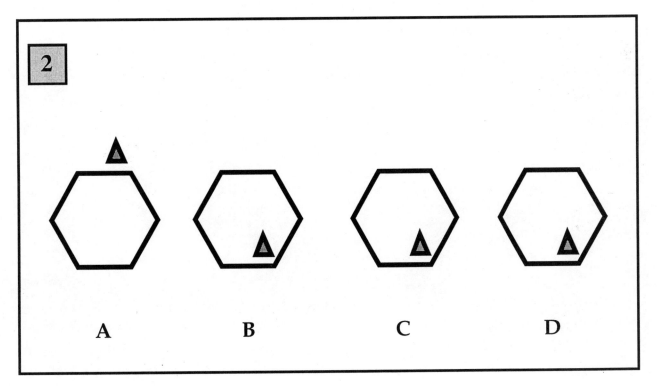

VISUAL SPATIAL RELATIONSHIP PRETEST

DIRECTIONS: Find the form that is different and circle it.

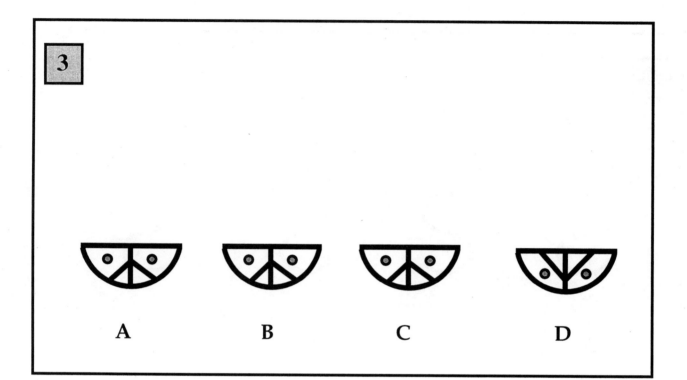

VISUAL SPATIAL RELATIONSHIP POSTTEST

DIRECTIONS: Find the form that is different and circle it.

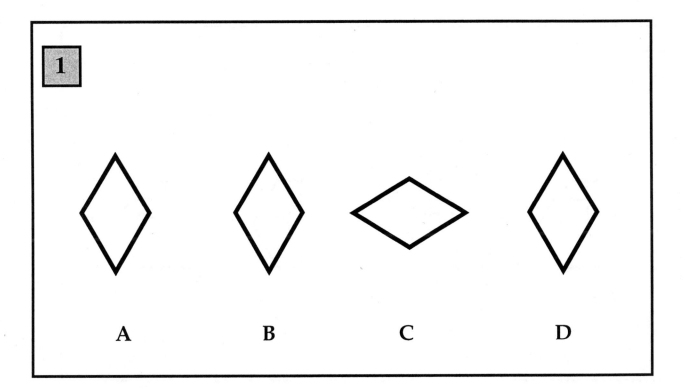

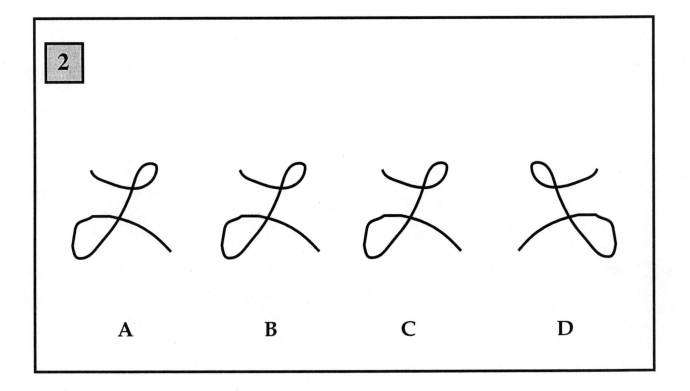

VISUAL SPATIAL RELATIONSHIP POSTTEST

DIRECTIONS: Find the form that is different and circle it.

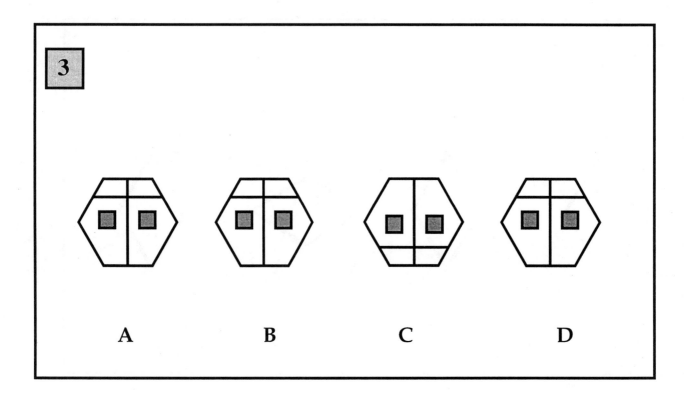

A   B   C   D

FINDING THE DIFFERENT FORM

DIRECTIONS: Find the form that is different and circle it.

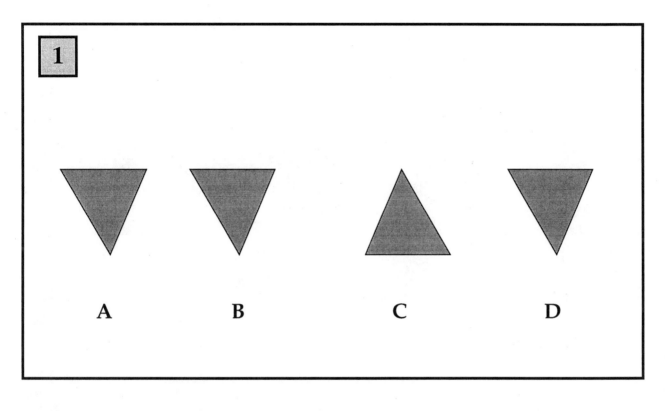

1

    A   B   C   D

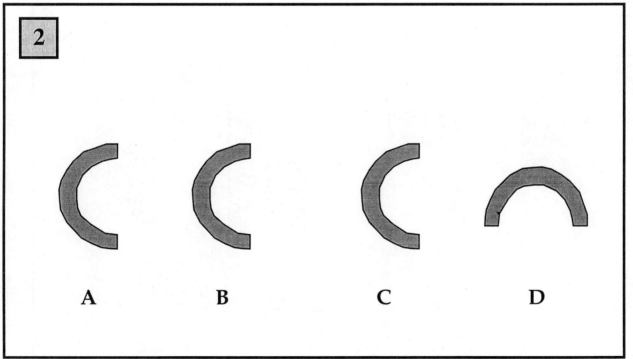

2

    A   B   C   D

FINDING THE DIFFERENT FORM

DIRECTIONS: Find the form that is different and circle it.

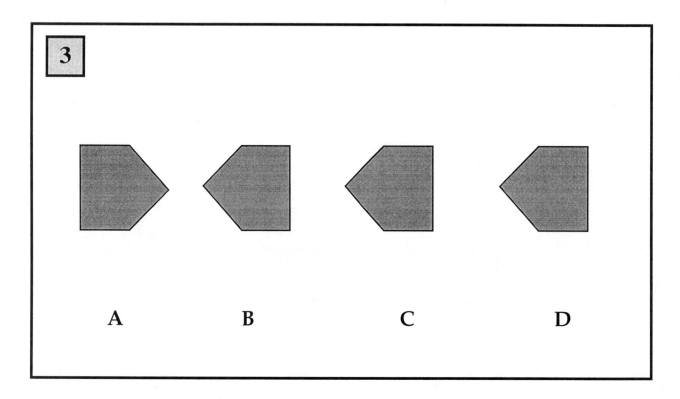

A　　　　**B**　　　　**C**　　　　**D**

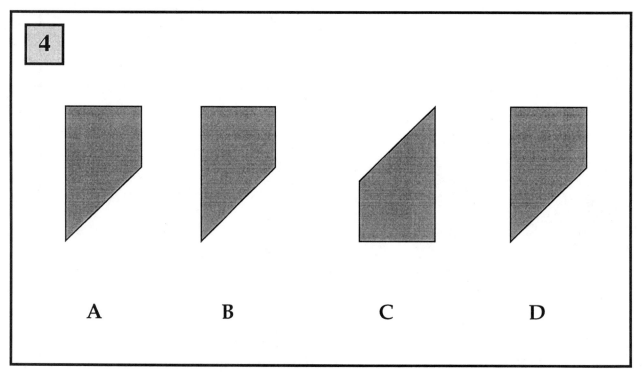

A　　　　**B**　　　　**C**　　　　**D**

FINDING THE DIFFERENT FORM

DIRECTIONS: Find the form that is different and circle it.

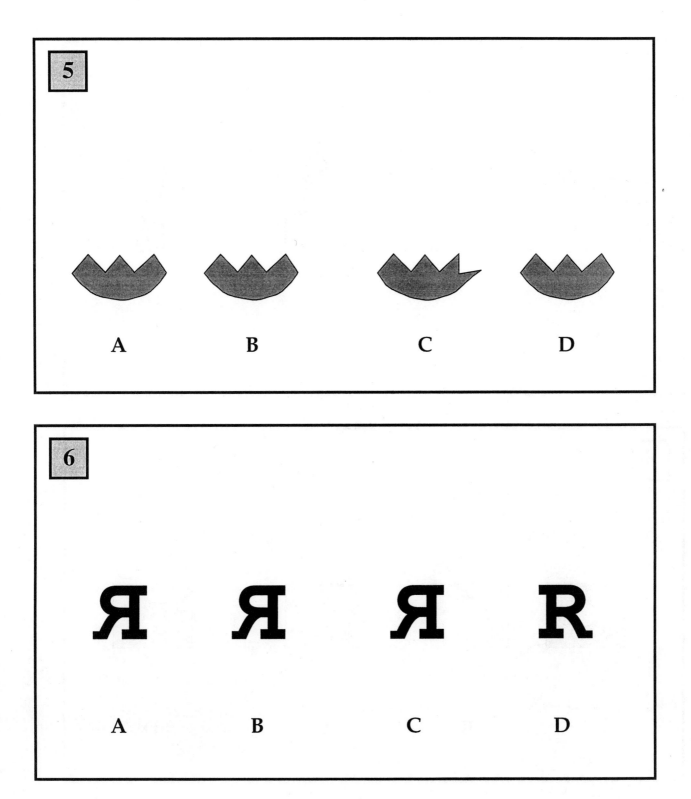

FINDING THE DIFFERENT FORM

DIRECTIONS: Find the form that is different and circle it.

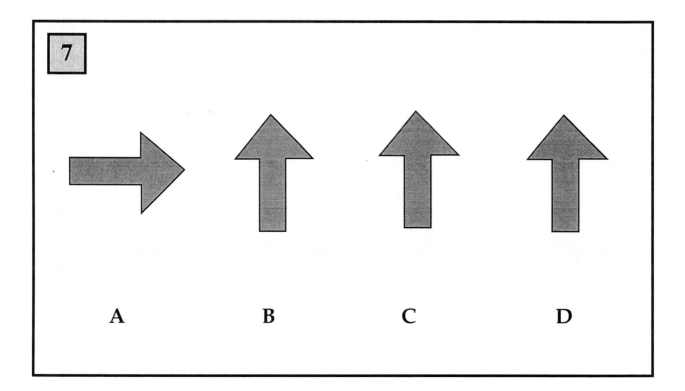

A   B   C   D

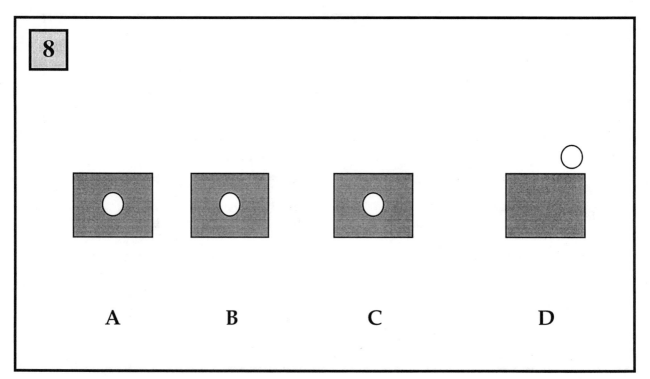

A   B   C   D

FINDING THE DIFFERENT FORM

DIRECTIONS: Find the form that is different and circle it.

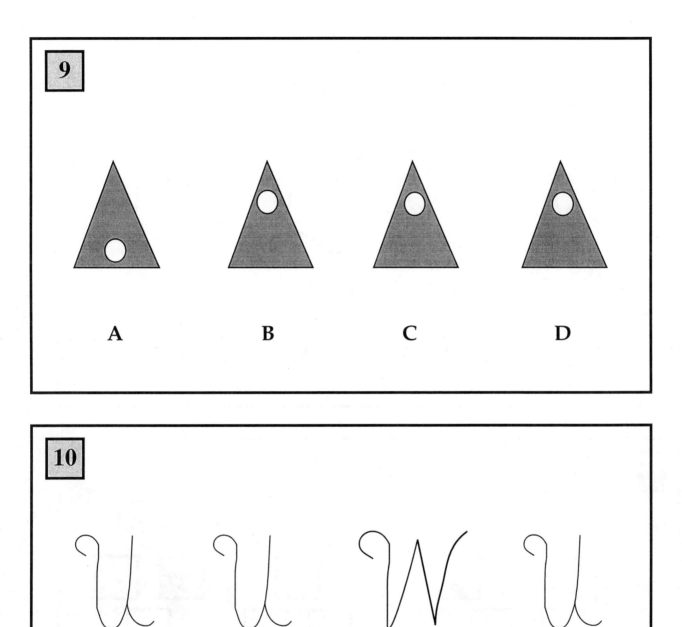

FINDING THE DIFFERENT FORM

DIRECTIONS: Find the form that is different and circle it.

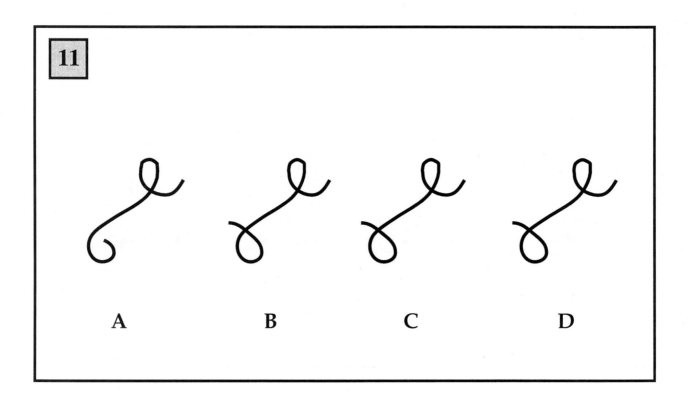

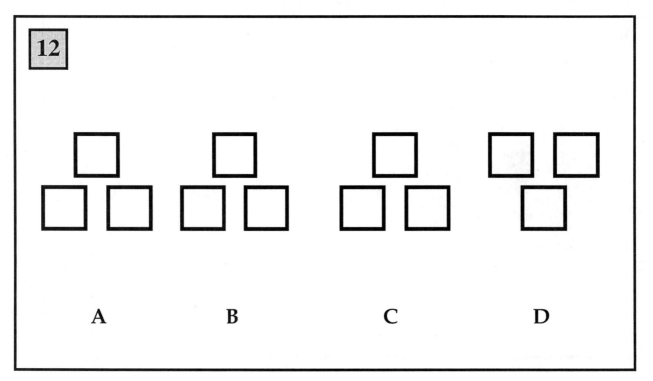

FINDING THE DIFFERENT FORM

DIRECTIONS: Find the form that is different and circle it.

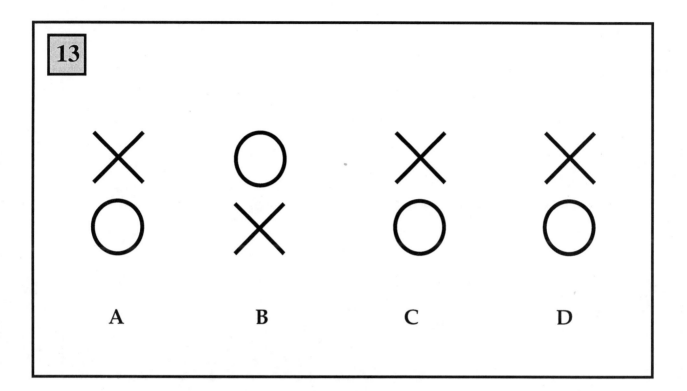

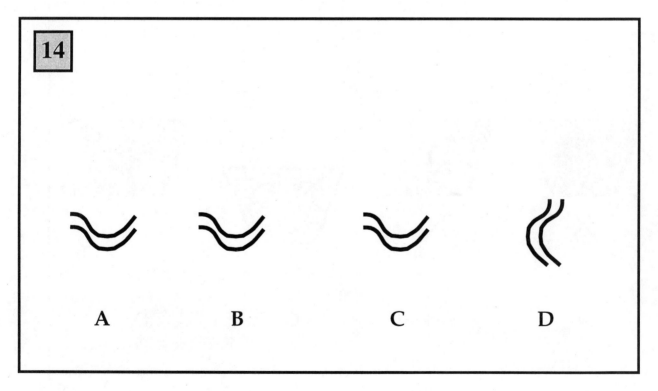

FINDING THE DIFFERENT FORM

DIRECTIONS: Find the form that is different and circle it.

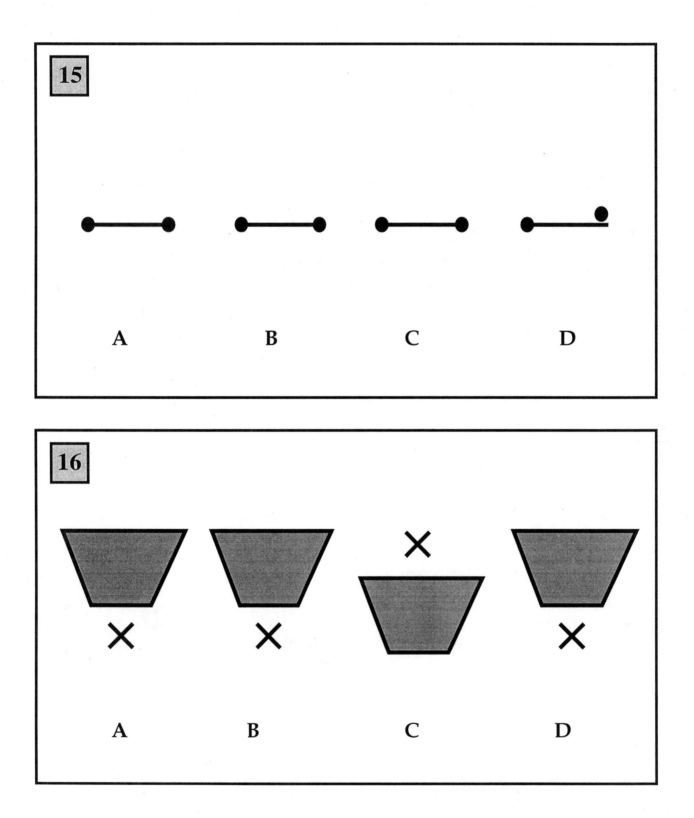

FINDING THE DIFFERENT FORM

DIRECTIONS: Find the form that is different and circle it.

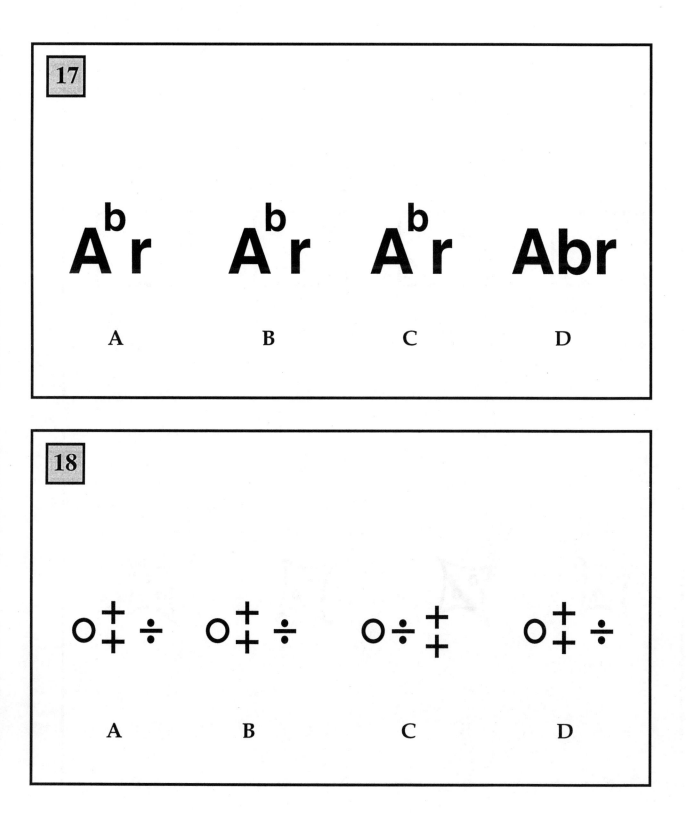

FINDING THE DIFFERENT FORM

DIRECTIONS: Find the form that is different and circle it.

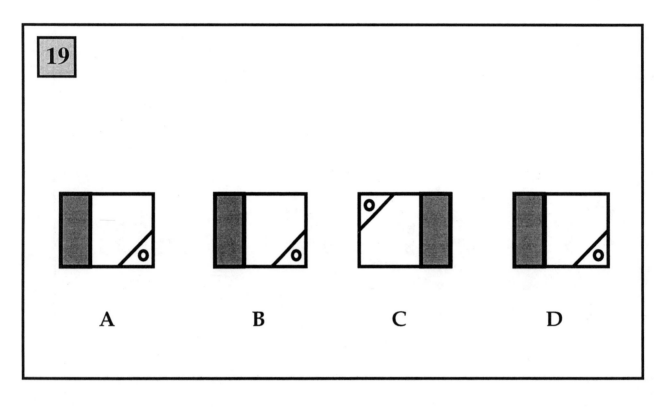

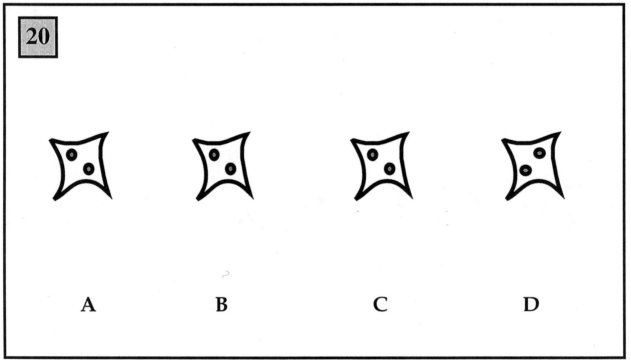

MAZES PRETEST

MAZES POSTTEST

MAZES EXERCISES

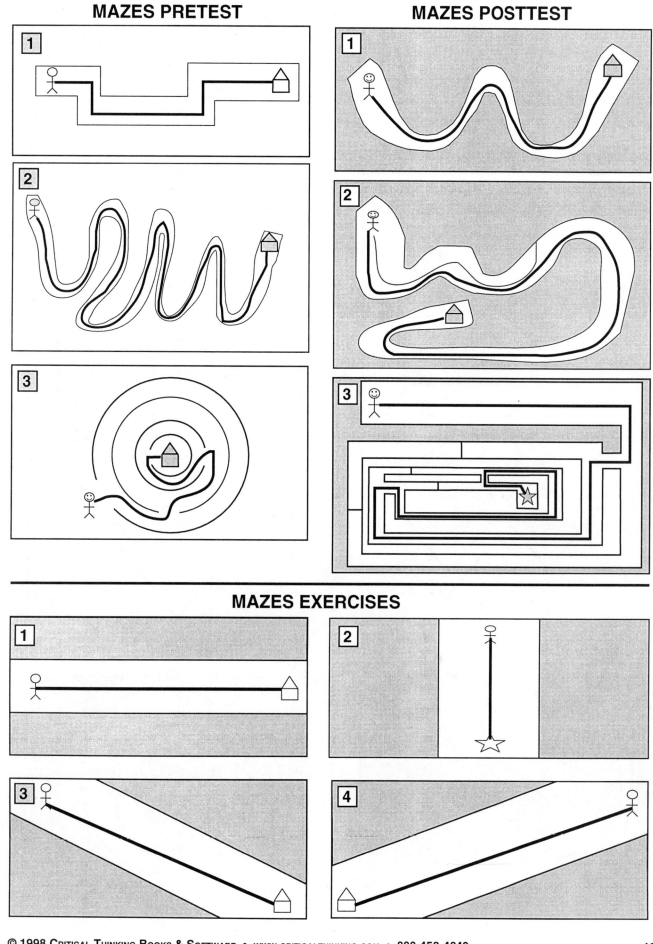

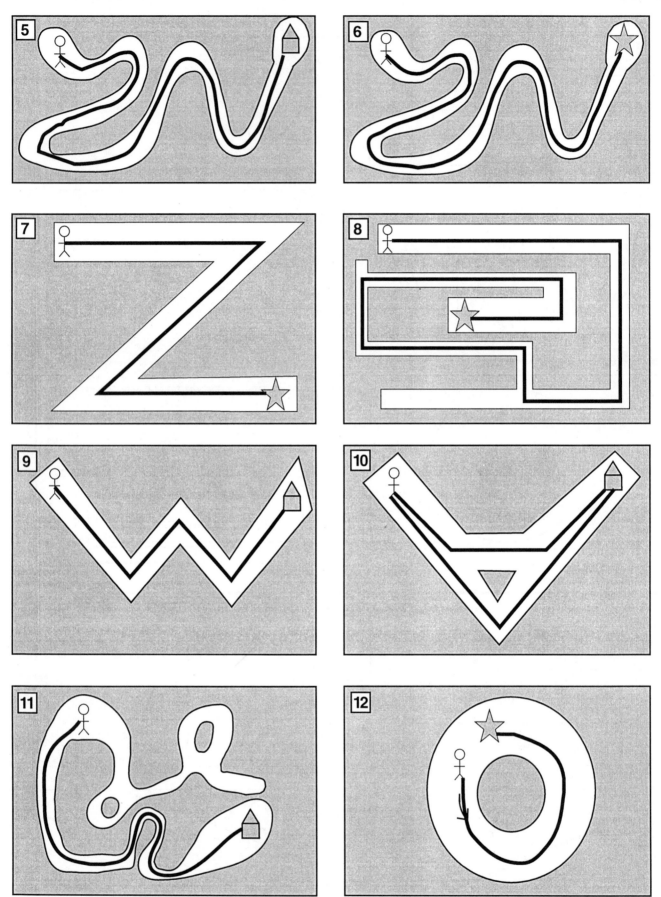

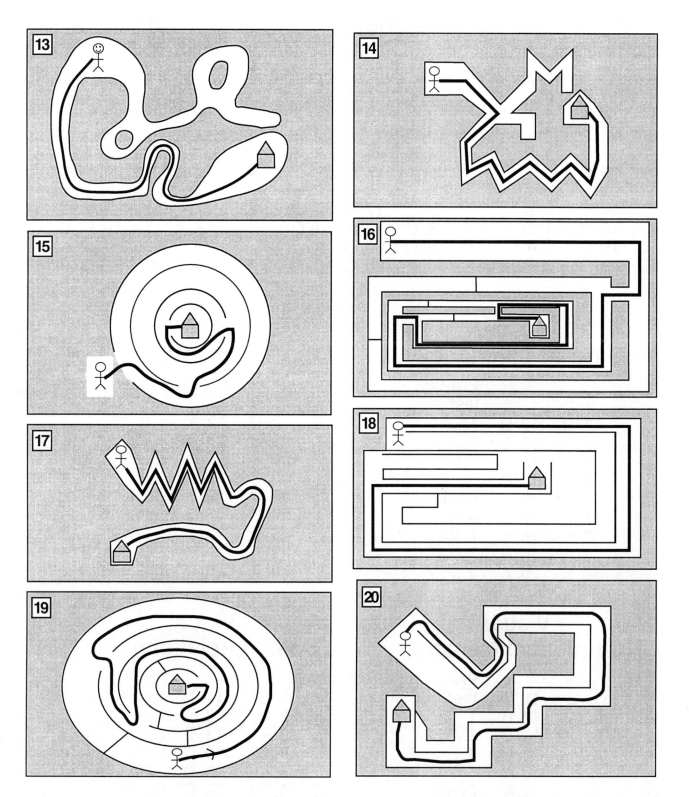

Visual Discrimination

		Pre-test
1. C	11. A	
2. B	12. B	1. C
3. A	13. D	2. A
4. C	14. A	3. B
5. D	15. B	
6. D	16. C	Post-test
7. C	17. B	
8. A	18. C	1. D
9. B	19. A	2. A
10. D	20. C	3. C

Visual Closure

		Pre-test
1. A	11. A	
2. B	12. C	1. A
3. D	13. D	2. B
4. B	14. B	3. A
5. A	15. C	
6. C	16. B	Post-test
7. B	17. C	
8. C	18. A	1. D
9. C	19. D	2. C
10. A	20. C	3. A

Visual Figure Ground

		Pre-test
1. B	11. D	
2. C	12. B	1. C
3. A	13. B	2. B
4. A	14. A	3. C
5. C	15. C	
6. B	16. C	Post-test
7. C	17. C	
8. A	18. A	1. D
9. B	19. B	2. A
10. D	20. A	3. B

Visual Form Constancy

		Pre-test
1. D	11. A	
2. D	12. D	1. C
3. A	13. B	2. A
4. C	14. D	3. D
5. C	15. B	
6. D	16. B	Post-test
7. B	17. B	
8. A	18. A	1. B
9. C	19. B	2. A
10. B	20. A	3. D

Visual Memory

		Pre-test
1. C	11. D	
2. C	12. A	1. A
3. B	13. B	2. C
4. A	14. A	3. B
5. C	15. C	
6. D	16. B	Post-test
7. D	17. C	
8. D	18. C	1. D
9. B	19. D	2. B
10. A	20. A	3. C

Visual Sequential Memory

		Pre-test
1. A	11. B	
2. C	12. B	1. C
3. B	13. D	2. A
4. D	14. D	3. C
5. D	15. A	
6. B	16. A	Post-test
7. C	17. C	
8. C	18. B	1. A
9. D	19. A	2. C
10. C	20. C	3. D

Visual Spatial Relationships

		Pre-test
1. C	11. A	
2. D	12. D	1. B
3. A	13. B	2. A
4. C	14. D	3. D
5. C	15. D	
6. D	16. C	Post-test
7. A	17. D	
8. D	18. C	1. C
9. A	19. C	2. D
10. C	20. D	3. C